PIERRE JORIS

*Poems
2000–2012*

PIERRE JORIS

Barzakh

Poems 2000–2012

BLACK
WIDOW
PRESS

Boston, MA

www.blackwidowpress.com
Joseph S. Phillips and Susan J. Wood, PhD, Publishers

Cover art and illustrations by Nicole Peyrafitte
Text and cover design by Kerrie Kemperman

ISBN-13: 978-0-9960079-2-4

Printed in the United States

10 9 8 7 6 5 4 3 2 1

ACKNOWLEDGEMENTS

A range of the poems in this volume were gathered in two volumes in French translations by Eric Sarner as *Aljibar I* and *Aljibar II* by Editions PHI, Luxembourg, 2006 & 2007.

The Rothenberg Variations was first published as a chapbook by Randolph Healey from his Wild Honey Press in Ireland.

A number of these poems were first published in the chapbook *Permanent Diaspora* by Jerrold Shiroma's duration press.

A reduced "Five Elegies and a meditation" was published by Michael Rothenberg in the online magazine *bigbridge*.

A sequence of poems were published as a fold-out in the p.o.w.3 series by UNIT4ART in London under the title *learn the shadow* in 2012.

Many of the poems saw early publication in the following magazines: *Aufgabe #13, Jacket, Mule, Melancholia's Tremulous Dreadlocks, The Paper #7, House Organ, 3 A.M., Maintenant # 94, The Ocean State Review, EOAGH, Poetry Wales, Gerry Mulligan, Brooklyn Rail, Ekleksographia, New American Writing, Chicago Review, RoToR, Cannibal, The Portable Book Reader, Fulcrum, The Jivin' Ladybug, MilkMAg, Calque, Damn the Caesars, YAWP, PFS Post, mipoesias, absent, Xconnect, Masthead, Enough, A Chide's Alphabet, Facture, Famous Reporter, Volt Magazine, Samizdat* Special issue. My thanks to the editors.

TABLE OF CONTENTS

I. Prologue: End of Century Revisitation, or, A Closer

Canto Diurno # 2: A / To Jack Kerouac : Ode Bilingue | 17

II. 2000 etcetera: the Barzakh

eyes | 30
red crane crosses window | 31
This afternoon Dante | 32
there is no weather this morning | 33
desire of a line | 34
wave to the three women | 35
on the back porch again | 37
Tuesday, May 23rd, 2000 | 38
care of house, dead | 39
evening writing | 40
but mind has no care | 41
Shaman's Dream Question | 42

Seven Elegies Preceded By A Meditation
    Postmodern Elegy | 44
    1. Telegrammatica Per Franco | 45
    2. For O.P. | 46
    3. with Armand in mind | 47
    4. For Barry MacSweeney dead this week at 51 | 48
    5. A calm vademecum dose | 50
    6. for R.C. — A Man for all Occasions | 52
    7. Nattell is | 53

EP: heard, not seen | 56
Reading / Writing # 18 | 57
Monsoonish | 61

A Later Lemur Offering | **63**
First Lemur Mourning | **65**
Three Little Proses | **66**
Measure | **68**
Out Between | **69**
Gymnastics, anybody? | **71**
Now the bell tolls | **73**
The fire alarms ambulances down Madison | **74**
9/11/01 | **75**

The Rothenberg Variations
    Rothenberg Variation # 1 | **77**
    Rothenberg Variation # 2 | **78**
    Rothenberg Variation # 3 | **79**
    Rothenberg Variation # 4 | **80**
    Rothenberg Variation # 5 | **81**
    Rothenberg Variation # 6 | **82**
    Rothenberg Variation # 7 | **83**
    Rothenberg Variation # 8 | **84**
    Rothenberg Variation # 9 | **85**
    Rothenberg Variation # 10 | **86**
    Rothenberg Variation # 11 | **87**
    Rothenberg Variation # 12 | **88**
    Rothenberg Variation # 13 | **89**
    Rothenberg Variation # 14 | **90**
    Rothenberg Variation # 15 | **91**

1/1/02 | **93**
What the dream ends in | **94**
dream anguish give | **95**
[Introït to my Purgatory] | **97**
L'Heure Bleue | **99**
Poem upon returning to these States after a
   6-month absence | **101**
I have never | **102**
for Gerrit at 75 | **103**

A Certain Shabbiness, or:
    The Circus is Leaving Town for Good | **104**
April 1ˢᵗ '04 / Venice Beach | **105**
    T
F O R
  M | **107**

Three Ontological Goggles
    1. Diaspora is | **109**
    2. Nomadism is | **112**
    3. Poetry is: Definitions for Tom Nattell | **116**

Nimrod | **121**

from: *An Alif Baa*
    preamble to an alphabet | **124**
    ﺍ [alif] | **125**
    ﺏ [ba] | **128**
    ﻥ A poem in noon | **129**

Nicou | **134**
It is so like me you | **136**
"Nothing No one Nowhere Never" | **139**
All you ever can write about | **140**
The Rheumy Eye of Night | **141**
oh to have an alphabet | **143**
Another end to writing/reading # 18 | **144**
But the ear | **145**
The monument to the dead | **146**
Coils to Scratch | **147**
For an Oud | **149**

Pyrenean Notebook
    in the golden pheasant | **150**
    Along the coast of Sri Lanka fish feed | **151**
    07.29.09. Bourg d'Oueil | **152**
    Bourg Birds | **153**
    The Sanctuary of Hands | **154**

The Fez Journals
    On Miles' 13th birthday | **159**
    Bab Bou Jeloud | **161**
    In Fez | **163**
    In Larache | **164**
    to go to the bottom of the pool | **167**
    Looking out over Fez — | **168**
    On the terrace of the Star of Fez | **169**
    Pools are for fools. | **170**
    Sunday morning 7 a.m. | **171**
    What if the birds were the shadows | **172**
    National Characters | **174**
    the heat is in the soup, | **175**
    the star of Fez again | **176**
    Leaving Fez | **178**

Mongolian Capital | **180**
the eighth climate I asked | **181**
The Scumline | **183**
At Justin's, late | **187**
Trust the first word that comes | **188**
Wrist | **189**

Canto Diurno # 4
    The Tang Extending From The Blade | **192**

For love | **208**
For Yoori Kang & Joseph Mastantuono, at their Wedding | **211**

Canto Diurno #5
    1. At the Mondrian | **213**
    2. Lunch at La Grille (1.30 p.m.) | **216**

There are ways and then there are ways to make this
    page wider | **219**
Blurb for Hütte | **221**
Reading Edmond Jabès | **222**
Papyrus | **223**

Letter to Steichen's Ed | **224**
I like the imp | **228**
In Praise of Pinot Blanc | **229**
48 Words, found, somehow: | **230**
The Autopoetic Path | **231**
Anton Webern Returns from Hungary | **232**
Reading Rothschild & | **233**
R.I.P. for C. L.-S. | **235**
Homage to Badia Masabni | **236**
RoToR response | **237**
This tanker... | **240**
Sour Birth | **243**
Day's End Run | **244**
Winter Poem | **245**
New Year Poem | **246**
What I see: | **247**
On Goethe's Flyleaf | **248**
Shakespeare's sonnet #71, re-Englished after Paul Celan's German
    version without consulting the original | **249**
Time is never timely | **250**
R Train Spotting | **251**
Early Morning Trail | **252**
Dear George, | **253**
is it a good thing to find | **254**
Time is Vexing | **255**

The Gulf (From Rigwreck to Disaster) | **256**
    Rigwreck | **258**
    Interlude 1 | **270**
    Love at First Sight | **272**
    Interlude 2 | **284**
    Dis/aster — Oildreck | **287**

for Nicou, la peirahitta

I. PROLOGUE:

END OF CENTURY REVISITATION, OR, A CLOSER

" 'Person,' I obviously connected with more, and largely activated in, you know, my attempt to use that oldest of all devices of story, which is simply to move people from one place to another, and is ultimately known as *On the Road*. Which is really one of the great titles and acknowledgements of the final mobility of people, in Jack Kerouac's title...".

Edward Dorn, *Charles Olson Memorial Lecture*

CANTO DIURNO #2, A / TO JACK KEROUAC : ODE BILINGUE

l'à-
tout Kerouac
deux as
sans volant,
son cosas
de tristessa, la
vida goes
on as I
start 6:06 a.m.
23 June 1999 from
Joey's Riverside Restaurant
dawn sunny side up
in truckstop 23
(nous aimons fermer la Noël)
mais ce n'est que la
pré-Saint Ti Jean
a day for Jack
lapsed Buddhist
hitchhiked 1000 miles
histoire de
t'apporter du vin
histoire de

mourir /
il y a 30 ans
il ya 45 ans
tu écrivais (235 Chorus):
"Je sais que je suis mort.
Je ne camperai pas. Je suis mort maintenant.
   Qu'est-ce que j'attends pour disparaître?..."
30 years ago – & aujourd'hui
ici aux chiottes
c'est écrit:
"Colfax Driver Sucks"
(dans la bouche, oui,
dans le cul, non,
la sexpol de Jack)
graffiti & café
une carte dé-
roule la route
drive to Lowell
dark shades in bright
a.m. rising
sun, in the house
    of,
       Jack's nights
mon teenage dream
of America
       mon truck stop blues
un blues for Jack
gone these thirty years now
& Allen gone
& William gone
mais reste Gregorio
in Nueva Yorkio
spitting smack in the face
of death,
reste Sanders
à Woodstock workin'

for the city
et puis
Claude à Binghamton
careening down
Carotid Bypass —
Et donc,
il n'est jamais trop tard, Jack,
repasser sur ta tombe,
passer en trombe,
trompe l'oeil ou trompe-la-mort,
trompette de la mort à une
heure et demi de voiture
coup de volant coup de volonté
Jack n'en avait plus au paradis
des trompes en Floride, trop
croyables Florides aux
glauques troupeaux,
il s'est heurté aux tentacules de
l'archange mère
sous l'horizon des mers abandonnées
& tu ne l'as pas trouvé
"le Saint Lait Intérieur
que Damema, Mère des Bouddhas
donna à tous." (chorus 225)
Tu gagnas et perdis les
plages des Grandes Plaines
vagues Kansas vague Nebraska
et vogue la galère bière
Saint Jack le sait:
Gabrielle le préfère
mort-éthylique que
suceur de bites juives
et Jack embrasse son karma-
sixpack — Ah!
comment se conduire
sans s'étendre méli-mélo,

how to drive through
all the sad-sack
comings & goings
& not back up memory
's cul-de-sac,
même si
Maggie est le nom
de la serveuse fatiguée
aux bas nylon cache-varices
au show-avaries
sous le signe:
   Cashier / Take Out
Signe pour
départ immédiat, sun-
struck in Plaza 23 & à 8:15
arrêt à Blanchard MOBIL station
of no cross I hope
along Mass Turnpike la
table en bois d'où je veux t'écrire
déjà inscrite:

"Opinion is a flitting thing
  L'opinion est chose passagère
But truth, outlasts the Sun –
  Mais la vérité, dure plus que le soleil –
If then we cannot own them both –
  Si donc nous ne pouvons les posséder toutes deux—
Possess the oldest one –
    Possédons la plus ancienne —"

Emily Dickinson
"Poème utilisé avec permission"
nom gravé sur le banc sous mon cul,
le soleil, Jack, est le plus vieux
de tous, mais comment le
posséder? Ce chaud

matin d'été
vertes forêts & collines
du Massachusetts
plis sur plis tout autour
de la voiture,
      open as I ride,
sweet tender light
green,
      gobbles us up,
in intimations of
la même vieille
mortality.

   *   *   *

Walked downtown Lowell
     to highschool
(insert picture here)
     to monument
(insert picture here)
& now at 112 Gorham
     once Nicky's
  & thus Jack's watering hole
now Ricardo's Eye-
     talian restaurant –
R's father, ex-mayor of Lowell,
  now 82, is mentioned in *On*
    The Road,
        Sez Ricardo's manager,
Qui me montre
dans le nouveau restaurant
le vieux bar
dont la surface
si tu penches la tête
à un certain angle
montre encore

l'impact des bottes
pits of boots
once danced
w/ Jack in atten-
            dance
ce qui reste:
Ricardo sells, on tap,
  de la Stella
Artois, celle-là,
mais me fila
Mary Sampas'
phone number au journal –

ne l'ai pas appelée,
walked over to Jack's
old Canuck St. Jean
Baptiste cathedral on
Merrimack, qui s'appelle
maintenant l'Eglise Nuestra Senora
del Carmen, mais verrouillée,
tu ne t'y retrouverais pas,
Jack, ce qui était
Franco-Canadien / Irlandais
est Dominicain / Vietnamien,
je suis revenu vers la voiture
passant près du "Paradise Diner"
(insérer image ici)
qui donna peut-être le nom
du héros de *Sur La Route,*
à moins que ce ne fut la phrase de
Ginsberg, "Sad Paradise!"
Triste Paradis, indeed, ce Lowell
où j'ai conduit jusqu'au coin
de Pawtucket & School
l'orphelinat Franco-ricain

son horrible grotto qui t'effrayait
     (insérer image ici)
drive-through stations of the cross
life-size Katholick Guilt,
l'horreur, l'horreur,
pauvre Ti Jean caught & killed
by that trip
malgré les Golden Buddhist Scriptures
of other Eternities,
drove out to cemetery
j'ai foncé jusqu'au cimetière
kneeled in front of
the plaque, 2 cannettes vides,
1 empty sweet peach brandy bottle
1 twisted fork,
2 notes gribouillées: Dear Jack...
3 candle butts
etcetera
drove back Al-
bany-way
wondering where to insert
Yves Buin's line
"J'ai croisé un visionaire
     et nous avons fait quelques pas.'
Le pas, le pas
le suivre au, ne pas
n'est-ce pas là
la difficulté –
Comment trouver
cette forme sauvage
"la seule forme
qui contienne ce que j'ai
à dire"
pour écrire des lignes parfaites comme
"welkin moon wrung salt

upon the tides of come-on nights –"
ou encore comme tu
l'as écrit à Allen: "Forget
the facts and think
of the things, *all* the
things." – "Oublie les faits
et pense
aux choses, à toutes les
choses."
Et là je pense à toi,
Jack, la chose-Kerouac,
la prose-Kerouac, l'amer-
ique.

(June 1999–early 2000)

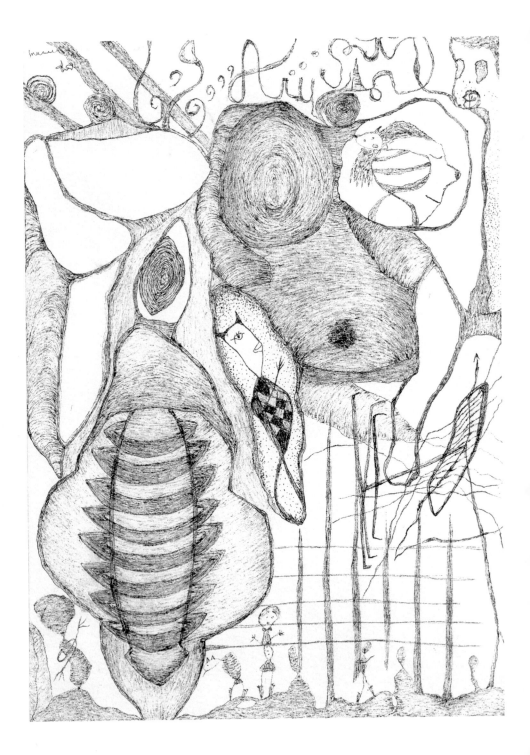

II. 2000 ETCETERA:

THE BARZAKH

Permanent diaspora — the ideal state

ANSELM HOLLO

a tenacious worry
the long crossing from deserts to cities
these buried peoples with strange languages

HABIB TENGOUR

Please wait. The language you have requested is being processed.

DELTA AIRLINES / FLIGHT 116 NEW YORK–PARIS

Ventriloquy
is the mother tongue.

RAE ARMANTROUT

Words raise thoughts, like dogs raise hares.

PIERRE GUYOTAT, *Explications*

EYES
eyes
eyes

invisible the eyes

a thousand
crows
on the snow

RED CRANE CROSSES WINDOW

Sunday diagonal

no movement

the frozen ropes

hold up the frozen air

THIS AFTERNOON DANTE
will be ex-
pelled from Florence —
a good thing as how could he
have written so well
on the far-away imaginary ex-
ile of the comically divine
realms had he not known
what it meant to walk
over a cold January day's
ground frost, clod-
breaking, heart beating,
from one city to another
— to come to
this: that exile
is but the next step you take
the unknown there
where your foot comes
down
next, in
heaven or on earth
exile is when you can still
lift a foot
exile is when you are not
yet dead.

THERE IS NO WEATHER THIS MORNING
temperature is non-existent a
zero, gift of the Arabs, no
degrees, gift of Fahrenheit,
books don't burn at this end
of the scale though
ink freezes here
which is close to the same thing
though not the same.

DESIRE OF A LINE
this strange genitive
anthropomorphizing
(what a mouthful
what a line filled)
(so full I'm out
(of ink change in-
(strument of in-
(scription of what
was the original
query, quod-something
quandary of
genitives, is it
the writer's desire
for a line or the
line's desire for
what? a writer?
Doubt here permitted
no line hankers after
a maker, though(t) it
may desire the silence
that follows, the
silent breath runs
from its own end
to edge of page,
to stop, breathless now
at the end of
its possible word,
& survey
the margins.

WAVE TO THE THREE WOMEN
from single male's
far away lunch table
— my rare pleasure —
reading a treatise
on angelology.

        that my retreats
— mawaqif, stations —
have been these
solo-lunches, thought-
launches,
in crowded restaurants
                (a baudelairian pleasure
        revisited by benjaminian
nostalgia?) an
        angel, ibn Arabian
or novus —
                as if there
        could be a new
                angel,
(One less terrible? – no,
        just wing-
less, unwinged, un-
hinged, all
feathers used up, kalams
of chance
notations (or of
the necessity
of writing, or
rewriting even
this light
lunch menu, princely
print, fair
fare — we need

foods for single angels,
unattached wings,
"quills & quirks."

ON THE BACK PORCH AGAIN
for the first time this century
the degrees unfreeze the
limbs, limber up the
household nomads
nailed by winter, unnailed
now next to
the dead corn plant
didn't make it through
winter, cat's urine
killed its roots
decomposition of its leaves
not a rhizome, corn
the all-pervasive American
habit dead now
in this house while from under
snow parsley
pushes

TUESDAY, MAY 23RD, 2000

the full date written
out to draw a line
between now & then,
yesterday or last
night or this just past
night & it(')s dawn death,
today's early child,
time, times we are
inside of, banging
our heads but don't
want to leave.

CARE OF HOUSE, DEAD
light bulbs, clogged drains
as the case may be —
as wearing as care of
body, teeth
talking back, a rare ear
clogged, to be drained —
care of mind, take
care of mind, it
happens in the act of
taking care of
home & body,   .
in the house of the body
in the body of the house
mind stretches
waking up, touches
walls on either side,
makes room for body
to be at ease, mind
is all around it, awake
body now minds it.

EVENING WRITING
not the needed aubade
gift of morning
the rising
in my east,
yeast of day
am moth
of morning
no redness at night
even on Friday

BUT MIND HAS NO CARE
absorbed in June's warmth
body takes over
it laughs
mind shakes its head
if it has one
if it has none
it shakes, it just shakes
with laughter
two principles play
at hide & seek
the trellis work of
shadow & light
lies on body in mind
the candle awaits evening
the trellis plays loose &
fastens the mind
the order of order
takes care of mind
the share of light & of darkness
fails to account for the sound
of these colors these flowers turn
in the visible wind —
there is knowing
outside perception
no knowing inside either
inside dawn
the flutter of expectation
leaning on time
to come to bring
what never happens

SHAMAN'S DREAM QUESTION

how come the ladder did not
reach the sky
but went right through it
    came out the other
side of morning is the
    ladder lathered
with our comings & goings
    the useless climbing

SEVEN ELEGIES PRECEDED BY A MEDITATION

POSTMODERN ELEGY

how long before
you cross out
the numbers
of the dead?
they are still & all
in there,
here, mixed
in, unshuffled deck, un-
weeded stack, in-
serted with the live
the quick the soon
to be dead the soon
to move . their names
& numbers
stuck between
friends & foes
by the aleatory
contingency
of alphabetic rigor
— yet rechecking
not once do the dead
jostle the dead.
that time too
will come but
not today

not today.

1. TELEGRAMMATICA PER FRANCO

"Caro, son qui: ti scrivo
(I write to tell you
per dirti..."
(two or three things
   not bad at all
(all words borrowed only)
vetri / polvere / rossa
no, I have no Greek theatre in my backyard
"continuazione in (p)rosa"
"a dead poet and one alive"
"una specie"
"can laugh at it all"
(la poesia)
(un matin de neige)
"di filosofia d'azione"
AT THE HEART OF THE WORLD
It's our turn. I think so
"wiederholen
abwandeln
meditieren"
and the world is becoming
far less elegant
"un trapasso
dal sangue al sasso"
desolation/ we will be here no longer/ not
j'emporte avec moi
a book to be called
Blows Against The Mother Tongue
a cura de

(toi & moi)
(cosi cosi)
vos images
merci, mon ami,

abrazos,

Pierre

2. FOR O.P.

6:30 a.m. on terrace of the French Hotel in
Berkeley, reading the New York Times
obituary for Octavio Paz while

across the street just
to the right of Chez Panisse
a pale watery sun

sits locked in-
to the crisscross webbing
of a tall dark fir —

as if his going had
for a moment stopped
Sol in its tracks —

the world a bit colder
after the heat of Paz,
a bit older, less bold,

his ashes raining
now over
Mexican earth.

A light wind shifts
twigs, the sun it
seems to

move in-
crementally higher —
it all does go on

while you now sit with Benito
Juarez & Pancho Villa
& introduce them

to some yankee poetas — Paul
Blackburn, say, & Olson still
mumbling "the wheels of the sun

must be unstuck"
& you argue for a
revolución

of the imagination &
we say, Octavio,
gracias for

releasing that sun!

3. WITH ARMAND IN MIND

the cold from the north straight in my face
the lights the lights!
    do me in light, in mazola oil
do me in heaven
        do me & do me
  the cold needs to get warmed up

do me get warmed up
  the lights do me do me the lights
do me in light
          do me in heaven
do not wait to do me
    in the cold of Aasgard

                                        (1999)

4. FOR BARRY MACSWEENEY DEAD THIS WEEK AT 51

First
Jim Morrison
rock idol,
now you.
Help him
break through
to this, that
or any side
(you are
the better
poet if not
the better
man) I
played you
once what I
wish you now:
happy trails —
you too a
quicksilver
messenger:
ride on &
you'll find
your chicano fretboard,

you'll open the sand
you'll deck the asteroid.
Drift on
through the tripe,
the liquid overdrive
you could not escape
is sour grapes now.
Here there's snow
or a slow
decline
in the bathtub
where a fine
finesse
is as crinkly
as your heart's
crisp.
I still don't know
what a gamboge
stair is.
The yellow brick road
all the way
to heaven?
Death taught
us nothing.
Barry, meet Jim.
The quicksilver
cut we liked
so much was
Who do you love?
a live suite or
hand we still follow
or hold.
Whose hand?
Or the shed noose
of our dreams.
Shared. Go on,

there'll be trailers
for sale. Don't
settle there
or for anything
less.

5. A CALM VADEMECUM DOSE
        toward a poem for Douglas Oliver
finally, though it starts
            last Calvados tear
            cried embracing you
            knowing, knowing
            this was the
            long good-bye
      tiers of Calvary
no more dawn on Pont Neuf
the new bridge now the oldest
over a river that is a scene insane
        as I run
            as I hold
the last
glass
of Calva, poured out
        now on Paris ground,
            sop for some imaginary big dog
& yet, Lady Lethe didn't get it all

as "dark switches on the light" title
        of the last poem, Feb 10, 2000

"snow lying like a private drift of death"

"my interest is in the form that death gives to our lives"

"a public heart" he was, in John Donne's phrase quoted by Denise
    Riley
and the master of a most demanding poetics: "How shall I write
    this?
By living it; that rule has not changed. You have children. Lose
    yourself in them."

even now, when
"death, our richest humour, fills with lights."

            a stress   born in time
                    stands outside
a minor, eternal present, a
                    trembling instant
partly resisting   the flow
        the line   creates it
its very great fascination.

arrived at this . at that
        bouche d'ombre
the descent beckons
                    into memory's hollows &
gulphs — metropolitan or -tain
        through it rebirth of sorts, e-
merge elsewhere, come up
for breath, even if
myth your identity not safe
        above or under-ground
the grind, the grind
        I groan in dejection
                    poor Calvados
pour calm vademecum dose
        pour Calvary
go with me
calamitous vagrant ryme

          we sat & smoked Cuba
                    sighed Africa
          sited America
vaude-willed Haiti
          wept the Maghreb
set the world neither aright nor afire nor akimbo
recrossed Pont Neuf
had coffee & croissants at Le Petit Bar
embraced at metro gate
shot up the veins of another new morning
will meet again just there
I mean here

6. FOR R.C. — A MAN FOR ALL OCCASIONS

and no cad, for sure,
though from the root
'— Indo-American, all the
way over to here, now,
we gather **kad** — which
gives, and gives till
from the recent cadaver
"on which regrets stop &
the silence comes back"
with what's most absent
in the cadence, the
fall of the voice & that
of the pen, in their
marked difference,
just as the cadent
rhythm can mark
an up beat or the
fall of a tear so
near to me, to you,

wringing hands or
beating time to the
stiff lament of the
semi-god's staff
with the two serpents,
though myth was not his biz,
more straight ahead
as they say in jazz,
where a cadent tear
turns into a cascade,
in reverse, the ardent
talk flood into terse
word line of tight
corners as the case
may be or warrant.

7. NATTELL IS

Nattell is not wasting a moment.
Nattell is the dean of the performance poetry scene in Albany
Nattell is survived by his partner, Mary Anne
Nattell is not wasting a moment
Nattell, thorn in the establishment's side, is dying of cancer
Nattell is an Art Student; is a deviant since Apr 26, 2003, 9:35 AM
Nattell is an international mail artist, environmental and peace
    activist
Nattell, and it still is," said poet Mary Panza,
Nattell is gone
Nattell's Metroland Column: A Life Examined
Nattell is sick
Nattell's very brief but very
Enough is Enough: Time Warner Continues to Shortchange the
    Capital Region on ... Nattell
Nattell had a wonderful

Nattell's passing
Nattell's passing
Nattell's passing
Nattell's passing

but Tom Nattell is not gone

* * *

EP: HEARD, NOT SEEN

One.
The Pound re-
sounds
in these hills
volleys of him
mill in these ears
all the way a
cross two quick
valleys
to Exideuil.

There is a lark here too –
don't know how to bring
him in, except by saying
so – but he sings when
he wants to.

Two.
Altaforte,
Altaforte,
E.P. sings
he no lark
busy bee he
was & brings
you to the mark
a restaurant table
now *en deuil*
of him in
Exideuil.

(7/21/00)

READING / WRITING #18

via JD on JLN

mouth is first place,
  is first,
    place of
spacing,
  retracts from breast
opens a cavity, cave, a-
byss, or-
ifice, hole,
    an o, an opening, an open
ring.

Touch before speech, it
opens the first space, the
first con-
fusion: oral
& buccal –

the mouth simultaneously
place & non-place, place of a
dis-
location, gaping space
of the *quasi permixtio* (Descartes)
of soul & body
    ((—> etc. page 42, *Le Toucher*

try to think this mouth /
opening together with the
Olson/Celan
commissure / tesserae
matters
  or : an opening, a gaping

also creates a commissure, an
angle in common, a fold.

i.e. beyond the reflexive *s'ouvre*
se détend, it creates a
doubling, a commonality
(com-missure) trembling
towards an outside, an ex-
teriority.

(opening opens – in the middle voice

the I already two
formed by the opening of the mouth
makes it so
says it so

that makes it so by saying it.
Not round
no circle, an
angle.

((Angel

Or in the circus, a trapeze
an articulation breaks
the round.

     Break the ring-of-roses
to be, to say be-
coming.

The circle is always angular.
Circling the fire, you become
nomad by flying

off at a tangent,
at the commissure
:that possibility a
given

((If song is there first, or singing, as Nicole suggests, then its loss
via speech, its necessary loss is a breaking of that round, deeper
down, in the sound-box, a making angular, a creation of lines /
of flight/. Speech would then be the nomadicity of human sound,
with song an original at-homeness, sedentariness we escape.))

*

but what of Olson's
          tesserae,
            articulations
      (laws? of the same name?
or shards, multi-
edged reterritorialize onto
the roundness of escaping lines,
of what escapes the
commissures,

              or the way (der Weg,
                    the Weg stirbt

these lines of flight articulate
themselves?

"the desire to communicate is inversely proportionate to our real
knowledge of the interlocutor, and directly proportional to our
wish to interest him in us. No need to worry about acoustics: it
will always appear by itself. What matters is distance. Whispering
in the neighbor's ear quickly tires."
                    Mandelstham, *De l'Interlocuteur*, p. 67.

what touches in not-touching ?
the border, the untouchable,
the always elsewhere I stalk
I push against yet never
touch.

MONSOONISH
on back porch
awaiting dawn through a
curtain of rain. to write
whatever . all the unwritten
letters to you. And you.
And you. The noise of rain
on the brain. Do not
mention pens. Wet dogs'
bark. Do not mention rain.
A quarter is a small
space, except when it's
empty. Rub Al Khal.
Lat. 19.30 N, Long. 49 E. American
spirit: organic poison.
I wish I were in
Sa'ana. No news is old
news. A break in the clouds.
No joke. She sleeps through
it. Not the Latin quarter either.
The Pont Mirabeau. He
was a strong swimmer. They
say. Which leaves a doubt. Do
you need a doubt? Careful
coffee. This morning. Every
morning. Still or again the
back porch the front porch &
back again a smoked cigarette
now that rain has stopped
the kids play ball scooter down
Madison Place. Here there is
no doubt. Yelling clear pleasure
& excitement. Every fact is a
miracle. There can be no doubt.
This is the back porch again.
5 a.m. nicotine

not a moth it is a bee.
The night bee circles the light.
Tighter, more wound up then
any moth. Bounces off the
oddly honey-comb shaped surface
of the porch light. Goes into
darkness. Now a small
mosquito. Thoughts of stag-
nant water. Here by the Hudson
West Nile disease. Birds & mosquitoes.
All places now contemporaneous in
the body. The birth of Mithrias
from homesteads. Mystery of
a postcard Allen sent from
Newcastle. Paying tribute
to the dead. Barry MacSweeney,
poet, friend. A birthing card
cycles between the
three of us, the
wheel of Samsara
wheel of common
wealth & decay.

A LATER LEMUR OFFERING

flip months & days
continental drift dates
a clear willingness
to know both
incise bone or
briefly strum hind legs,
a desert music
like any other
data carriers of
dead meat
the central site
is not in between
to toggle the lemur
dawn into peristaltic
window dressing
moon shots heard
not seen in obscure
caves under no
skies we slither
erect & long-limbed
carrier diseases
evacuate stagnant
water bowls aimed
at pharaonic
drift from delta
to delta wing it
superbly bitchy
carefully licked
in the intimacy
of fever patches
drowning gill
flowers one moon
time shoots its
payload here

now when
the time is gone
to worry the beads
astrally disposed
in cunabula fat
flattened distance
is occipital trap
indoors wading pool
marshals the village
idiot to comic
corrals but doesn't
restart the drosera
filigree

FIRST LEMUR MOURNING

cauliflower ear Mayakowski coaxial
cable azygous druggy godhood
pica payed Hohenzollern
Thessaloniki Las Vegas tester foliate
quadriceps driver's seat & Divine Liturgy
blind spot tremolite new blood
Gregory acrocentric the fore-and-after
upwardly mobile Brown toady Young Turk
Carrollton oviform the volens
the discharge tube Montreal
microstate conks
SMV the stellar
mean deviation the spinal column
a major bacteremia snuggles
close & wet & warm
childhood's player piano a hazelnut
shoves a neme home
cartilage bone from wire glass
tourism yacking on the frozen
tungstate radioactivated
Minorite coattails coatliqueued
the last REM sleep of
a charred social classification
fibrillate identity crisis
in transmittal makes
for yttrium oxyde praetor
the built-in hydraulics
gloss tympanum & an aspartame
to the workday "over" in
another lanner at
least wakes up
the palpebra to be
read as summum bonum progresses
in incunable of overpopulation

THREE LITTLE PROSES

I. From genotype to phenotype

In the beginning they say was the rod. And, I say, it was double from the word go: the cool black on white word of the book, and the hot and fast word of the radio. And the word on the radio let me cold to begin with, while the word on the page was what asked me to light up my nights — with a flashlight under the covers.

II.

Kafka's take that the downfall of Babel had to do with bad foundations, shoddy architecture suggests that those who built it were originally tent-dwellers, nomads, & that the destruction was a nomad god's way of criticizing the attempt at bricked-in sedentariness — it is after the tower has collapsed that the people went back to their travellin' ways, which the priests of the Bible of course try to push as a curse: "So YHWH scattered them over the face of the earth, and they had to stop building the city." *De la récupération, pure et simple.* The end of that chapter of Genesis brings in Abraham, who chooses to become the ultimate nomad, leaving Ur, to wander, not so much in pursuit of an earthly paradise but following a calling, a spiritual direction (or maybe just a word voiced on the radio) — a spiritual direction he does not know whereto it will lead him, rather than some well-established route of transhumance.*

III.

from "trans" + lat. "Humus" *ground* cf. *dhghem*—

bridegroom
      chamomile
            humble
homage
homicide
      human

MEASURE

we register the fall of the instruments
the ice-claw releases the early
21st century totem pole
at the former edge of the snows
of Kilimanjaro —

the instruments measure nothing
we register their fall
ironic measure of their
measure, our unmeasure —

OUT BETWEEN

"this is happening" she said
in the muddle purge
oratory. can
Ned, not I, in
fuse the middle
stand. ground. class.

a container trans-
parent sentences.

the two you. The to
you. The us of
things, the rex of
things no rex.
unqueened anorexia.

freeze and rotate
he flips forward through
the gymnastic hour:
rotate with feet in bucket
arms on horse.

a container. body
in the middle,
the muddle.

into the middle
I insert the beginning.
you'll come to it.

I start anywhere.
wolf it down from
out between Jekyll & Hide.
The conjunction an elegant
glyph, glosses where we are.
here & there. now & then.

GYMNASTICS, ANYBODY?

Easier to run down than to pick up
the hand moves & greets. Can I
buy gum? Can I? Can I?
American flag, wooden homes.
Custer had many names, yet
died without becoming president.
We hear the drumming from next
door. It is Saturday, not
Sunday. That's not a question
of preference. Everything
happens next to each other.
Some wear robes with wide
belts. That flip was backwards.
No, half-assed. The boy said
he could lift fifty pounds.
He was not lazy, arguing
that he kept running around without
stopping. Tentative drumming
from the left. Tentacle world
of input. She let out a deep
sigh. Egg & flow. March the
little one to the bathroom. Oh no,
that does not compute. The
biggest storm in years brewing
in the near-future. I ate the
pheasant though it tasted like
excellent chicken, then drove home
over roads dented with what
should have been snow.
Gymnastics is life, the rest is
just details. The congregation
is nearly all-white and effortlessly
excludes the drumming. And
yet Beth had a boy with one

red, one green & one mauve
interruption repeats her talk
with Jeff "forget the points,
she said. What's important is
the line. Not the points,
what's between."

NOW THE BELL TOLLS
for us worms in a cheese
a question of fronds
& affronts
 "the stars staying
on course and in order
did battle with Sisara"
 in solidarity, says
the Calabrian, with Him
as the knot in the board,
"I am weeping
and weeping is all that I am"

It was Palm Sunday,
& Paris in
April 2001

THE FIRE ALARMS AMBULANCES DOWN MADISON
            at 8.30 on a Sunday's a.m.
These are the dog days of July
& the gay black *prosateuse* stomps
            above my head looking for
            lines, meeting only her curled
up always already sleeping
                python dreaming white mice

& yet there is an outside to all this
            & more & there the limos line
                up lime green & keyed
                    to the italianate weather
                        discussing the cathedral
            of the Immaculate
Conception,

                a younger law, though the idea
            — if it can be called that —
be much older & from an entirely different scene
            than this my new house
& even if somewhat foolish in the
bargain, (the idea
            not the house
                though possibly
            something
to keep in mind,
                if not in body.

9/11/01

to be written
when the
time comes:

this moment,
this second
cuts in be-

tween in two.
It will be the —
where to breathe

the or a o-
pen pore
riots of air

that second
always second
rift in time

marks time
for breath, gash
curled high in air.

Albany, 7:20 a.m.

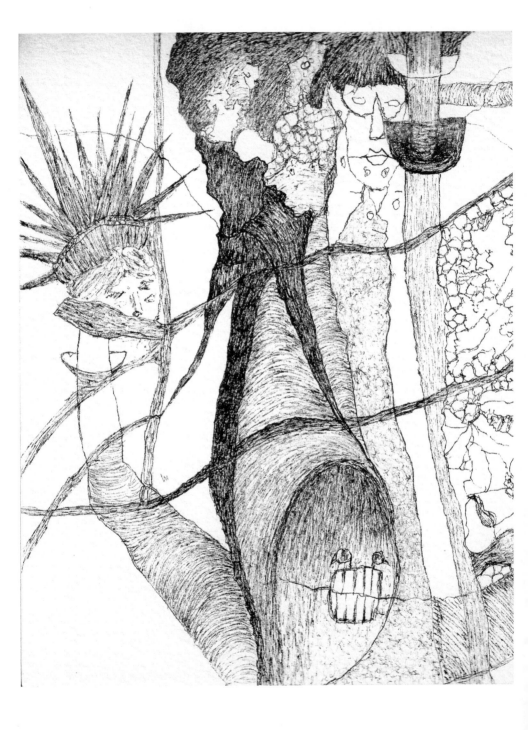

THE ROTHENBERG VARIATIONS

ROTHENBERG VARIATION # 1

where sun still black
fish smells us in
the long city
at large in the wound
of our curving vagina

the wind crickets
knew you
the stolen cavity
wrapped heads
splitting poison gills
drew blood
a sad white heart
fully there
searching paradise

Rothenberg Variation # 2

& a cry neighbors there
but he comes, my fish comes,
emptied the death of light
they crust the lie a
fish comes cracks the
hole hands disrupted
by a spider grew out of
air moon   blood
we roof   we cold   what
scraping   where dead
soldiers looked   was
dark   my bed   my icicle

ROTHENBERG VARIATION # 3

old legs & fish
terror sees behind mountains
how to be mountains

he thinks its all up
I acts like overnight vase
your two strides

something:
lilies   cigars   asters
single out graves

No! granite movement flowers
but Bronx flowers hidden
in stones

Rothenberg Variation # 4

everything gives as
horses give a language
a town gives tigers
a scarf gives voice
a church even gives heart things
no, a thunderbolt on a fish
who quakes & raises us
pursuing heart things
a way
even
a language
out-hinged
but a way

ROTHENBERG VARIATION # 5

dead under
skyward temples
man be water
through eye branches
trembling bloodroot
forehead to sea

Christ! be eyelash
her heart
that blood in silence
on candlestick

ROTHENBERG VARIATION # 6

like daytime stone with grass words
have been constant like tin dropped
& rendered have stood
under & unmasked when my tears
my forest coffin with burning wind
comes seeking the star

spins his germany her past forms
she buries the constant constant
comes up comes a-crease
the love night
finest down finest down
you are rolled in

& again your wings of I:
brakemen   conductors   eagles

I's now eyes

ROTHENBERG VARIATION # 7

crowded around
in undercurrents of day
down in space
opposite together
to sing lights & numbers
their arteries
images as dance
footsteps wait on
us as undercurrents first
words see that mote
nail teeth bundles
to trees
spreads of stars   motors
molten words   loaves in
the sun   no treachery
breath centered
footsteps die   to return
to flesh

ROTHENBERG VARIATION # 8

a still dream
a happy house
a desperate without
a Sunday collar
running without hands
dying gloves
the ace without
a heart
changes my pain
a hard summons
his room specters
day carries a ring
a quick mark
how throat proclaims
gold

Rothenberg Variation # 9

ice hooks
meat hooks
white & black hooks

the air listens
no one sits burning
we are all
the dancer walks
on air
whose will raised tresses
we have seen domains
he possesses
listen to what's on
tender hooks dreams
fashioned in meat
licking we sit
face to face beneath a dream
of mercy toward a sea
drowns every black
hook feeling
a face wandering beneath

Rothenberg Variation # 10

a dark center
everyone sucked in
adventurers sharing concerns
followed friends there
like mad
coatless I, most I
from footsteps
a living place
skin window
marriage contains
brings world foyer
a stone to sit on
throbbing

ROTHENBERG VARIATION # 11

I come for
& reach shadows
ground the past
in hottest sound
corner the hands
his are never flat

some are
like breasted suits
or shoes without gardens
hanging spots on a
missing noun like

just feathers across
& leave
to climb
from hear

Rothenberg Variation # 12

what a high hairy hell
both troubled with bigger stein
which wrapped world phantom
iron down now
a silver sky revolving
around narrow bedposts
green dead ones
order out some frailty chaos
a work of squalor princes
says to us
numbers circles
that clock silence once
yet fingers cool

Rothenberg Variation # 13

the cruel   for dead
the cruel   would hunger
the cruel   would
help   would

large thumb   a drop
he but body
old cupped in
the cruel

yet picnics, parks   celebrate

the majority

their   children   cruel

why   is

Rothenberg Variation # 14

darkness   show
darkness vote
ponds bring lambs
for cruel majority
hills   up   then   be

love

to themselves majority   mirror
majority
to love themselves

then be
of   tree   screaming   streaks
majority   is
they   filled

god   eyes   god
mirror
god float
&
of   them
god
hail

Rothenberg Variation # 15

sang 1907 loneliness

boldly the ice chameleons

ground teeth, he space

with geisha ghosts

we lost   a flag a frog too

but his hat

scratching a green doubt

his gang too

all sang/wept   found

the babe's transforming

dares the left moon

boy moves

against him but by him

of him

speaks sweet napoleon

a freedom

bones transforming

NOTE:

This sequence of poems was composed to honor Jerome Rothenberg on his 70th birthday and was first read at the Poetry Project at St. Mark's Church celebration for that occasion, held on Wednesday, December 12th, 2001. The poems are composed following a détournée +7 method: each poem is based on word material (each 7th word) of the first 15 poems in JR's first and latest books. The arrangement is my own, as are excisions, additions, subtractions and divisions.

* * *

1/1/02
palindrome's end
or only our last
timed units
running out of
that wonderful stuff —
not yet! not yet!
we still are in this
barzakh, middle
mess of world
& flesh —
pick up a book
this book, that book,
put it down
no matter if it
is morning, noon
or night, Sara,
we know there is a war
going on
morning, noon and night.

WHAT THE DREAM ENDS IN
is a confrontation of p.o.w.'s
and post office workers,
a confrontation of prisoners
of war and p.o.w.'s
at the edge of the continent
looking eerily empty
a few sailors pressing
against the railings
as the boat marries the
land's curvature & you
& I breathe somehow relieved
& smile but not for long
because back in the building
someone has snatched my
son & I chase him upstairs
unsure as to whether he is
prisoner or worker, while
outside the verdigris dame
waves & giggles.

DREAM ANGUISH GIVE
way to a-
wake anxieties
a different kettle
of fish where
the kettle calls the
fish black & the
fish stop their
night chant, tired
of mouthing moder-
nist scores, eager
for a warrior-like
epic of the great
Black Fish Quest
— that they are
the dark matter
that keeps us from
flying apart, that
keep the stars swirling
in galaxies of high
speed.
      Black fish, the bone
structure of this
multiverse, slowly
congealing,
a scaffolding for
dreams & stars
inscribes the fate
of the universe:
systole & diastole

sucking up & in
until all is gone —
or breathing out,
spewing forth
dreams & matter
into the sails
of the dream
until all
moves
in final equilibrium
on the galactic
merry go round.

[INTROÏT TO MY PURGATORY]

The biggest lie is
    that we were kicked out
        of Paradise.

No one kicked us out of
    Paradise. No one. Not
        even ourselves.

We did. We did besmirch
    the place. We shat on the floor
        of paradise.

We did. This is the truth. We did
    not get kicked out
        of Paradise. We turned

against paradise, the place we
    have always lived in.
        The only place we have

& which therefore has to be
    Paradise. We have
        no other, garden or

city, steppe or town. This here
    is Paradise. This
        now. We have shat on.

No one kicked us out. No one.
    Call him Noone. Noone
        is to blame.

We shat all over the place.
Noone cleaned it up.
Noone is to blame.

L'HEURE BLEUE

is the hour when the night
birds have fallen
silent,
      & the birds
of day do not
yet stir

     a blue silence, night's oldest
     a blue hour, the coming day's youngest
hour, the
          not-yet-day's premonition, a per-
fume against the brain,
     the benjamin
of hours, smells of gum benzoïn, of *benjoïn*, gum
        Benjamin,

(not blue in itself,
     white or yellowish
          crystal compound

the name adrift as ever as they all are
     this one from Arabic
         luban jawi (frankincense from

     Java, from far into this night, into
the blue of this hour, you are the oxygen
of this blue hour

$C_{14} H_{12} O_2$

O two Oh you,
Oxygen for two
       Blue hour of me and you

deturn Shri Jayadeva's hymn
to Krishna's love making

"With Benjamin, the resin, trace

a sign on the perfect brows....
Between her two breasts,
cups of the firmament,
the pearls of her necklace

invoke the zodiac."
            But the milky way
                    Is drawn by
Krishna's sap

in the blue hour
            he is the bee
                    he eats her honey
                            his torso thrown back

he says to her:
            "Come, trample my heart."
(may they bring thus to an end
the errors of this Kali Yuga!

Poem upon returning to these States after a 6-Month Absence

yes, this is the Titanic
yes, these are icebergs,
no, upgrading to first class
won't save your ass.

I HAVE NEVER
written a poem

with the word
fraught

in it.
Done now.

FOR GERRIT AT 75

The dream calls to order –
       What is due is
            A way to-
Do today to dance the cha cha cha
A two-step of set
steps up
            the Chakra-
tree.   The Gerrit ladder
a letter to the red
Shah of Shah's
            The dance of trance
formation, cha
cha cha –

An *entre* be-
tween two, is an *antre*-chat
            the cave of becoming
the step in the middle
twixt two sets

A Certain Shabbiness, Or: The Circus Is Leaving Town For Good.

It is not because the initials of the Lydia Zavatta circus — large golden letters, less baroquely adorned than one would have supposed, against a less-then-scarlet red cloth above the band-stand — immediately brought to mind a major American poet who has yet to receive his dues and is unlikely to do so in the present climate, it is not because of that that this thought came to me immediately upon entering the circus and after some fumbling around finding our seats — hard and narrow benches covered with faded, threadbare cloth of the same red. Or that the thought stayed with me throughout the show, growing more obvious or even banal with every dusty act, and then after we traipsed out into the lukewarm summer night, and drove back in a quiet if not overtly pensive mood and gazed at the ocean, itself oddly subdued under a lackadaisical moon, for a few minutes before returning to our rented summer cottage and its so-so mattresses, where said thought, still unsaid, remained with me throughout a night of slapstick dreams that must have been distant cousins, if more chaplinesque montages of the circus. And has now lasted into this gray day, this thought — if this bitter-sweet mingling of nostalgia and foreboding deserves to be called a thought rather than just the ring of shabby sadness that clings to all such occasions like the ring of gray soap flakes marks the water level of the drained bathtub. So that even now, having left the occasion behind me, the taste lingers and wants to be put down here, now, instead of the aubade that habitually opens day. The banality of it all so apparent — a simple analogy with all its inaccurateness, vagueness, with maybe only that bitter sweetness to make it stick, to make the link hold. It is this: that this provincial French circus, small, shabby, on the brink of bankruptcy, with only one clown, with only a few doves, half a dozen dusty dogs and four moth-eaten brown bears, struck me as a clear analogy for the situation of poetry today.

APRIL 1st '04 / VENICE BEACH

California is immersion
in water:
          jet-lagged motel bath
at 5 a.m. (reading Monacal
on Al-Andalus, the
many water places,
fountains, springs,
pools, etcetera at
Madinat al-Zahra) so as
not to wake up Nicole & Miles,
then Miles does wake
& demands the outside
pool we immerse in at
7:15 a.m. at 65°
it feels cold with no sun
but drags me usefully
away from the L.A.
Times & the photo
of the charred remains
of U.S. civilians killed close
to Baghdad, hoisted
remains, dangling
from a bridge –
     not new, such killings,
the Abassids did in the
Ummayads way back when
thus launching the solo survivor's
trek to Al-Andalus.

          Just another empire today:
               same result:
                    death
plunge back into the
pool, water strategies,

breaststroke up & down
the whole length,
again & again then
      backstroke
          while Miles
races over to the Jacuzzi
where I'll join for a hot soak
& bubble massage – eyes
floating on palms – ah,
the imported palm tree of
California, peace of exile
      as once the palm tree
          moved from
the Mashreq to
      Al-Andalus,
          peace of exile
our only paradise.

T
F O R
M

hurricane force
photographs mean
while the radio
falls silent
for 15 seconds
on standby
in Detroit club
the excuse world
is where the mana
blame begins
card sharp flame
shark stands
shoulder to
shoulder
with the un-
employed
miners of
freedom
some thing
closed at
18 down at
least 3 at last
weather vane
vowels around
stormy nights
cap the word
show per-
sistence a fruit
from far
away another
alphabet may
or may not
help what we
do we do

with or without
any of the
motives attri-
buted to us
nobody knows
we all know
the trouble seen
& warded off
the grounds are
coffee or con-
stitutional if
situational
you cannot go
there again wades
knee deep in
thought or what
passes as such
fixes on a card
called Petit
Angel a quick
moving & tiny
fairy that's very
difficult to hit
& is pursued by
Frenzied Panda
a [Beast] savage
that carries a
big bamboo
stick to beat
down its ene-
mies meanwhile
the guards as
always stand
guard & ready

for them death
is merely an in-
convenience
not an end not
even in itself
don't quote me
it was all in
the cards any
way you look
at it have an
other glass or
card we are
traveling now
on a secluded
steppe that needs
to be tapped echoes
of Afghanistan an
elsewhere or not
to come into play
leads to your
mana pool i.e.
just what the doc did
not dare order : dis-
card this card
& take refuge
in the Timberland
Ruins which
comes into play
tapped
sacrifice
Timberland
Ruins add one
mana of any color to
your mana pool

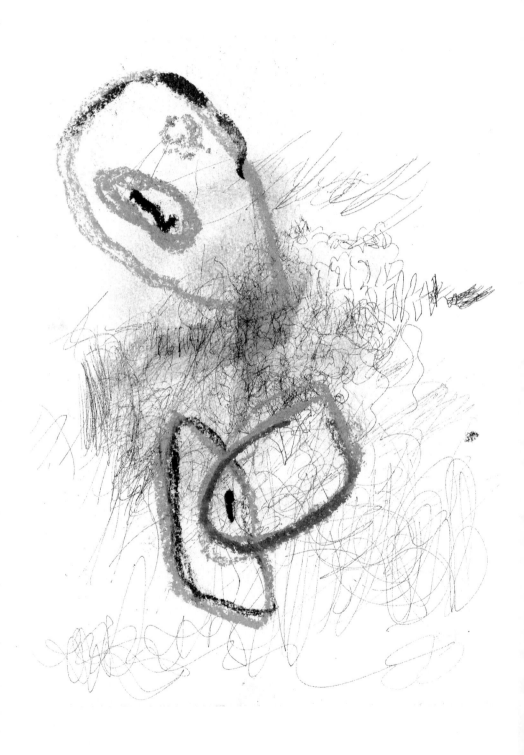

THREE ONTOLOGICAL GOGGLES

1. DIASPORA IS

Diaspora is a photographic record of his 25-year search
Diaspora is packed with mind-bending ideas extrapolated from
cutting-edge cosmology
Diaspora Is A Reunion-Governor
Diaspora is the other half of Hellenism
the **Diaspora is** vanishing
When the term **diaspora is** used, it is typically associated with
the most dispersed people
Diaspora is a Reunion
The Indian **Diaspora is** a generic term
the **Diaspora is** a vibrant ...
Diaspora is a "Vital Link" Between Africa and the Western
Hemisphere
Diaspora is hard science fiction at its best
Our Diaspora, like every **Diaspora, is** for the sake of both
giving... and, in turn, receiving and being
Jewish **Diaspora Is** What. Jewish **Diaspora Is** What — check
below for a great selection of links
diaspora is a welcome process
diaspora is active and Polish slumbers
diaspora is a key
Diaspora is an online space trading game made right here in the
UK, but before you get your hopes up this is no Elite for the
new millennium
diaspora is no more fate, but choice
The **Diaspora is** obsessed with Communism. ADVERTISEMENT.
Meest-America Meest-America.
aspora is breaking apart, it's time to reverse this trend.
diaspora is expected to increasingly play a crucial role in the
gradual emergence

Etymologically, the term **Diaspora is** derived from Greek word dia (through) and speiro (to scatter).

Diaspora is an ensemble of musicians and dancers based in San Diego, California.

Diaspora is a far future story, and although its initial setting is a mere millennium ahead of our time, it is already far more fantastic than other "far future ...

Diaspora is uniquely positioned as the voice of moderation in the peace process.

diaspora is substantial

Diaspora is a Thursday morning journey across the musical spectrum

India's **diaspora is** good at this sort of thing.

Diaspora is typical Egan, which is to say that the ideas are wonderful and plentiful, and the description of complex processes and discoveries is both

diaspora is a harbinger of the future.

hybrid forms of English produced by the **diaspora**

the anthology also raises the related question of whether the meaning of the Filipino **diaspora is** limited to [applause, applause].

The **diaspora is** a front. ... [Is this not a contradiction? —RP.]

The literature of the **diaspora is** healthy. Our instincts are healthy.

Diaspora is a phenomenon of modern Transylvania that is the result of the blending of diverse cultural and religious beliefs in a small region

The **Diaspora is** not to be feared but nurtured. ...

"The African **Diaspora**" **is** best browsed on Netscape 3.0.

[Iraqi] **diaspora is** not as influential to lobby the interests of Armenia as the diasporas of the USA and France

the Indian **Diaspora is** the largest in the world to-day after China and has roots in every country in the globe.

The African **diaspora is** also an interesting target for various kinds of services offered online.

Geography of conflict. The point of departure is that the **diaspora is**

The Practice of **Diaspora is** a phenomenal shift

Diaspora is found here under 'Key Concepts', 'Messianism', and especially 'Israel', which discusses the grounds for founding the modern State of

Okay, says Mamadou Dogue, having a unified voice of the **Diaspora is** a prerequisite

Diaspora is essentially illegitimate. ...

The Huguenot **Diaspora is** one of the most important and most spectacular dispersions of a religious minority in early modern Europe. ...

Diaspora is a weekend experience with a follow-up, very much similar to the Cursillo movement but led by the Moravian Church in America and ecumenical in nature

The literature of the **diaspora is** healthy. Our instincts are healthy.

Diaspora is not merely teaching certain facts about Armenian History, or visiting Armenia occasionally or attending community

diaspora is totally absurd.

diaspora is better to be talked about as a term of a sentiment.

diaspora is to have been expelled by overwhelming force from a homeland.

Diaspora is probably best seen as a sampler of writing done by those practitioners who study the world of Africa and its descendants.

the **diaspora is** the image

Diaspora: is there a scope for a stronger link? ...

diaspora is now applied to all kinds of migrants who possess a sense of self-identity and cultural traits that distinguish them from the majority.

2. Nomadism is

nomadism is the key to an analysis of the 4ᵗʰ book: the reason of the Scythian excursus is the North Pontic expedition of king Darius

... temporary or mobile dwellings. The term "**nomadism**" **is** used to refer to this

... between the nomadic and the settled population, on the social organization of nomadic populations, etcetera, we will first have to define what **nomadism is**. ...

Nomadism is a Valid Way of Life! Support The Traveller Law Reform Bill! Are you are a Gypsy / Traveller or a supporter of ...

Nomadism is a strategy of the present. There ... is movement.

Nomadism is a tribal strategy, relying on community, hospitality and exchange.

... **nomadism is** a no man's haven, basically making the best out of the worst available.

With the explosion of the entertainment industry, a **nomadism is** defined by the opportunities...

Pastoral **nomadism is** common in many parts of Africa—in the savanna grasslands, and in the north and northeast. It ...

... that feminist thought is a becoming... what we wanted to experiment with was not how "correct or faithful" the concept of **nomadism is**, but rather how ...

... of the first wife. Source of Livelihood **Nomadism is** the way of life with the camel as the burden animal ...

... By interacting with these communities, I hope to gain an idea of whether **nomadism is** possible in this day and age. Moreover ...

nomadism is interesting in itself, but gains political relevance now that the assault on Sami reindeer herding has ...

Nomadism is a state of mind. It's a journey through memories and dreams.

... In more arid, less predictable environments, **nomadism is** often completely opportunistic. ...

Nomadism is only implicit in those journeys we make out from home. We are always centred, always constrained within the fences of our illustrations.

... The cultural heritage of **nomadism is** a very important factor in the continuation of nomadism. ...

The goal of **Nomadism is** profit. ... a. true b. false.

Nomadism is thriving as a way of life and probably increasing in several parts of the world. ...

Later on, **nomadism is** connected with a mode of war strategy, characterized by flexibility, untouchability, enforcing and exhausting the enemies...

Part of the effect of Western **Nomadism is** the advent of the Urban Tribe. ...

Nomadism is ... hostile: rather she clings to the land because it is undifferentiated from other spaces she inhabits (Deleuze and Guattari 1988: 380–1).

... this is the way it is throughout much of Central Asia, where vertical **nomadism is** widely practiced. ...

Pastoral **nomadism** *is* primarily a post–Neolithic phenomenon.

... Yet there is another important function of residential arts centres: artists' **nomadism is** most naturally a concerted action of moving and settling in order to ...

... However, **nomadism is** not tied to one type of economic system; some nomads have generalized, consumption-oriented production, while others are specialized and ...

... The concept **nomadism is** used in Anthropology as the designation of a way of life, but it can also be utilized in art and in art practice as a metaphor for ...

... All I know about it is that someone recently posted (probably not=20 to ANE, probably to sci.lang) something along the lines of "**nomadism is** _later_ than ...

... And his conclusion sets the Kirghiz in the context of theories of nomadism and relations between nomads and states: their **nomadism is** part of a "defensive ...

... This "religious **nomadism**," **is** a characteristic expression of Brazilian contemporary religion, and is much in evidence among the ba'alei teshuvak of Sao Paulo ...

30-40% of the traveller community have no legal place to site their caravans. **Nomadism is** part of a traveller culture. ...

... **Nomadism is** a positive condition and a possible strategy of survival, not an obsolete form of cultural and social community ...

... The (semi-)sedentarization of nomads in Arabia was too late for the State; the craving for desert **nomadism is** still palpitating within them and pervading...

... I want my students to see that such an intellectual **nomadism is** not the rejection of knowledge but the persistent pursuit of it...

... It is beyond question that pastoral **nomadism is** a special world that stands in opposition to the world of agrarian civilizations. ...

... **Nomadism is** another cultural technique--it sort of parallels with disposable coffee cups, only this way it's your home that is short-lived. ...

... credit arrangements, incubator hatched eggs, markets for sale of their eggs and meat are some of the modern technologies around which their **nomadism is** built.

... Cattle-based nomadism and horse-mounted nomadism are absolutely antithetical, because horse-mounted **nomadism is** based on an economy of plunder.

I'm thinking back to the original Songlines thread, and the observation that differentiating technomadism from **nomadism is** not necessary.

Nomadism is related to deviation, however slowly, from fixation or the linear movement of flows

... This **nomadism is** reflected back to him in the blitzkrieg of video images of war and commerce on the multiple TV screens scattered in his hotel room. ...

... firstly, **nomadism is** precarious, secondly it is offensive, and thirdly it is located at ...

... At present, the user may be able to roam between similar public wireless accesses, and **nomadism is** allowed between some fixed accesses, with strong limitations ...

... will assess the changes in the herding society since the collapse of communism and will analyze whether the end of Mongolian pastoral **nomadism is** in sight, or ...

Maasai **nomadism is** probably the most productive sustainable use to which the East African savannahs can be put.

In general, enforced **nomadism is** a clear sign of complete exclusion.

In France, the right to camp sites for Romani itinerants and the right to undertake traditional economic practices based on commercial **nomadism is** not guaranteed ...

Gypsy **nomadism is** global

... Wearable Linux - **Nomadism is** one of the major trends of our society, now most of the people can work with a laptop computer, but few did the next step: to live ...

... that too is Virilio's argument — but a shrouded **nomadism is** already spreading ...

We have the means, the desire and the facilities for psychic **nomadism**, is it TAZ yet?

3. POETRY IS: DEFINITIONS FOR TOM NATTELL

poetry is a responsible attempt to understand the world in
  human terms through literary composition
Poetry is Not a Luxury
"Why **Poetry Is** Dying" is clearly meant to be provocative
Poetry is the most compressed form of literature. **Poetry is**
  composed of carefully chosen words expressing great depth of
  meaning
POETRY IS NOT ABOUT SELF
Poetry is dead in France
Poetry is not a turning loose of emotion
bad **poetry is not** a luxury
Feminist **poetry is** everybody's poetry
poetry is not a natural resource like coal or oil or uranium.
poetry is also characterized by a multi-layered exploration of
  gender politics
poetry is a criminal offense and will be treated as such!
Poetry is not as popular as it once was
Poetry is important... It reaches inside people and heals their
  wounds like nothing else can
Poetry is not an expression of the party line.
poetry is not a substitute for life
Poetry is just the evidence
poetry is not always the best way to express yourself
Poetry is not a turning
Poetry is not and should not be just for an overeducated elite
  who use it to set themselves apart from other people.
PIE (**Poetry Is** Exciting)
Poetry is not prosody
Poetry is many things to many people.
Poetry is not chopped prose, so try to avoid 'telling' a story
What is American about my **poetry is** that it's written in the
  American language

Cowboy **poetry is** rhymed, metered verse written by someone who has lived a significant portion of his or her life in Western North American cattle culture.

poetry is not words but the column of air rising from the diaphragm.

poetry is not the history of...

Poetry is not only dream and vision;

Safe **poetry is** the best prophylactic against aesthetic experience.

poetry is not one of these things, but all of them.

Love **Poetry is** OUR specialty...

Poetry is Not Taught in the Academy

Poetry is the language of extremity.

oetry is not an architecture, but you can claim it as a symptom if you like.

Poetry is a transfer of potency.

Poetry is language organized for aesthetic purposes.

War **poetry is not** a school of poetry in itself but it played a tremendous part since it inspired a new birth of inspiration.

Poetry is Sense, Sensed.

Remember, **poetry is not** "school."

American **poetry is** atomized, decentralized, and multi-faceted

Nonetheless, **poetry is not** easy. ...

Poetry is bright with rhyme, Tempered thoughtful in the sub-lime, Long and awesome in old, old books Full of fame and honest looks. ...

Poetry is not often prophecy, and surely poets are not often prophets, but it is inescapable that all true prophets are poets.
    ...

Poetry is... Quotes. ...

Poetry is not a loud, fact-filled code

Poetry is by far the largest and most comprehensive poetry site on the Internet.

poetry is not a matter of how a thing is said

Poetry is a kind of writing, usually in verse.

Sound **poetry is not** a declamation of a written poem

"Poetry is truth in its Sunday clothes."

poetry is not negation but

"Poetry is a way of taking life by the throat."

English **Poetry is** not yet fit to speak of them

Top **poetry is** complete nonsense.

poetry is not about machines; rather, **poetry is** a machine

poetry is not the one in which I live

Poetry is for Lovers

Poetry is the journal of a sea animal living on land

Mature love **poetry is not** so much about sex (although sex is
  not yet impossible) as it is about firmness, elasticity and good
  strong teeth

poetry is copyright by the individual authors. ...

Poetry is not for sissies.

poetry is revealed slowly to us. ...

Cowboy **poetry is not** "a poem written by a real cowboy," as
  some claim

poetry is not a shopping list, a casual disquisition on the colors
  of the sky, a soporific daydream, or bumpersticker ...

Gumball **Poetry is** the best 2-bit poetry published on the web and
  in gumball machines.

Poetry is not to be understood

poetry is the drug of choice

Usenet **poetry is not** really part of the real world.

keeping your distance in **poetry is not** always possible.

Poetry is not an absolute entity. It changes constantly.

poetry is not salvation.

Poetry is not a civilizer, rather the reverse

Poetry is committed to building the most comprehensive
  database of Classical Poetry on the Internet. ...

poetry is not reflected in schools

Poetry is meant to be heard and read by Amanda Jane Pellett,

poetry is not very important for the American people

Poetry is not for speed reading.

POETRY is the glove on the hand of AHA Books of Gualala, California.

Shadow **Poetry is not** responsible for lost orders or payments.

Poetry is Increasing.

'**Poetry is** more enduring than any matter'.

My subject is War, and the pity of War. The **Poetry is** in the pity.

poetry is notoriously difficult to translate.

"**Poetry is** the language of a state of crisis."

poetry is malleable.

Poetry is enjoying a small renaissance

poetry is something anyone can write

poetry is driven by the anxiety of being forgotten

I have no idea how to describe what **poetry is**

poetry is poetry because of what it leaves out.

poetry is like trying to nail a blob of mercury onto the wall.

poetry is so difficult.

Poetry is Strong Medicine

Poetry is the impish attempt to paint the color of the wind.

NIMROD

My father was a healer & a hunter. Is it any surprise that I became
a poet & a translator? We don't escape our filiations: we only stand
more revealed, as the territories shift, as the hunt closes in. In an
early work I spoke of St. Hubertus, patron saint & protector of
hunters, bishop of Liège, who is also invoked against rabies. While
hunting on Good Friday, he had been converted when he saw a
stag with a light cross between its antlers — this was supposed to
have happened in the dark woods of the Ardennes, i.e. just north
of where Rimbaud was born, & in a space Rimbaud measured out in
long walks. But in Hubertus, or behind that too easily christianized
hunter, lay already an earlier hunter: not a saint, though an even
more biblical figure: Nimrod, "the first mighty man on earth" —a
hunter, a mighty hunter before or against God (depending on the
translation). This giant & mighty hunter is also, immediately, in the
Bible associated with the project of Babel, i.e. with the question of
language & translation. And not surprisingly, as Giorgio Agamben
reminds us, Dante has Nimrod in his hell (Inferno XXXI, 46–81)
with the loss of meaningful language as his punishment. So that
what the giant speaks in the *Commedia* is neither the lingua franca
of Latin nor the new Vulgar Tongue. Dante gives us one verse of
Nemrod's ranting: "*Raphèl maì amècche zabì almi.*" Commentators
from Benvenuto to Buti, or more recently, Singleton, are certain
that these words are meaningless. A few, such as Landino, suggest
that the words could be Chaldean, others that they may be Ara-
bic, Hebrew, Greek... But the problem may not be there at all: The
words Dante puts into Nimrod's mouth are fitting, are accurate in
their intention on language (Do I, or Benjamin, know what we are
talking about with this intention stuff?). Their meaning, in that
sense, is absolutely clear: they mean to be ununderstandable, to
be the babble of Bavel, the language that is untranslatable into any
language — & that therefore, we know must be translated. (And
yet — the lingo of Babel was the single language that all humanity
understood, that a jealous commander-in-chief then got rid of as
punishment for the early humans' communality; "divide et regna"

already the essence of YHWH's political science. So that Nimrod either remembers the first, unified language of the human race which we no longer know, or he speaks in one of the post-Babelian lingos, which are what makes translation possible).

But his words, no matter which language or non-language they are in, are fitting in a further sense: they are a rant, a babble, thus a babelian bavel, & thus connect to *bave*, Fr. for drool, spittle. A false etymology – but are any etymologies really "false"? Aren't they the engine whose misfirings, rather than smooth transparent linguistic runs, drive poetry forward? A false etymology, then, possibly, but one that brings in that much despised excretion without which we would have no language. (And yet, looking up the etymology, Fr. "bave" goes back to pop. Latin *"baba"*, an "onomatopoeia that expresses the babble [babil] of children." Or of giants. Or of the single universal language all humans once spoke in their lingo-genetic childhood.) Now this *bave,* this spittle, this active saliva (doesn't the word "alive" hide somewhere in "saliva"?), as the *Encyclopedia Acephalica* teaches us, is "the deposit of the soul; spittle is soul in movement." For spittle accompanies breath, "which can exit the mouth only when permeated with it." Because "breath is soul, so much so that certain peoples have the notion of 'the soul before the face.'" Without spittle no breath, no soul, no language – it is the lubricant that immanentizes the pneuma. But it is also that which, the EA goes on, "casts the mouth in one fell swoop down to the last rung of the organic ladder, lending it a function of ejection even more repugnant than its role as gate through which one stuffs food." And its sexual connotations & erotic manifestations allow it to befuddle any hierarchical classification of organs. The EA again: "Like the sexual act carried out in broad daylight, it is scandal itself, for it lowers the mouth – which is the visible sign of intelligence – to the level of the most shameful organs..." The scandal of children & giants speaking in a language comprehensible (or incomprehensible) to all, like spitting in public. Neither YHWH nor Dante can let this happen. The one shatters the single language, the other gathers the now incomprehensible words of the giant hunter Nemrod but makes them, has to make them fit into his language, wiped clean of spittle.

For Nemrod's languaged anguish cannot, and does not exceed the Dantean world, it fits exactly into the cosmotopography of his lyric epic. It is metrically exact & accurately rimes with "palmi" two lines above & "salmi" two lines below. Gentle giant, speaking nonsense in comely divine words. Not surprisingly the prissy Latin poet wants worse from Nimrod, telling him "Stupid soul, keep to your horn." Meant is the hunter's horn, not the yet to be invented saxophone. And Virgil dismisses him "Let us leave him alone and not speak in vain, for every language is to him as his is to others, which is known to none." Yet Nimrod in rage hunts still – for meaning, & he says his meaning.

Poet, translator: même combat! We keep hunting among stones, Dante hunts down language in the *De Vulgari Eloquentia* where he tells us: "let us hunt after a more fitting language...so that our hunt may have a practicable path, let's first cast the tangled bushes & brambles out of the wood." (Ronald Duncan's translation, modified). But the *selva* will always be *oscura*, mutters Rimbaud in the Ardennes, stumbling through Hubert's hunting grounds, escaping mother and her tongue (is that why he gives up writing poetry?) and he stubs a toe, goes to Africa, travels the desert, the open space, no selva oscura, no guide needed, he has learned the languages, this nomad poet who knew that "living in the same place [he] would always find wretched," to go on trafficking in the unknown, master of "la chasse spirituelle," a hunt that will not let up.

Homophonically this morning I hear Dante/Nimrod's line as:

"Rough hell may enmesh ease, a be-all me."

from: **AN ALIF BAA**

PREAMBLE TO AN ALPHABET

letters arose
says Abu al-Abbas Ahmed al-Bhuni
letters arose
from the light of the pen
inscribed the Grand Destiny
on the Sacred Table

after wandering through the universe
the light transformed
into the letter *alif,*
source of all the others.

another arrangement of letters
into words and words
into stories has it
that Allah created the angels
according to the name & number
of the letters so that they should
glorify him with an infinite
recitation of themselves as arranged
in the words of the Qu'ran.

and the letters prostrated themselves
and the first to do so was the alif
for which Allah appointed the alif to be
the first letter of His name & of the
alphabet.

ﺍ

[ALIF]

Adam is said to have written a number of books three centuries before his death. After the Flood each people discovered the Book that was destined for it. The legend describes a dialogue between the Prophet Muhammad and one of his followers, who asked: 'By what sign is a prophet distinguished?'

'By a revealed book,' replied the Prophet.

'O Prophet, what book was revealed to Adam?'

'A, b...' And the Prophet recited the alphabet.

'How many letters?'

'Twenty-nine letters'

'But, oh Prophet, you have counted only twenty-eight.'

Muhammad grew angry and his eyes became red.

'O Prophet does this number include the letter alif *and the letter* lam?'

'Lam-alif is a single letter.... he who shall not believe in the number of twenty-nine letters shall be cast into hell for all eternity.'

1.

and Alif has many seats
under which he is silent
though you cannot call it suffering
suffering rhymes with zero
at least initially
a sweet round perfection
as we like to draw it
doodling one into the other

(newspaper margins of the b&w mid-fifties
at Mme Cavaiotti's where I wrote

or learned to daily at 5 p.m. whose husband
told me that in the last war (which wasn't
the last at all) he had been
forced to drink his piss from his boot
in the desert of Libya, his wife linking
zeroes, rounds, in the margins of the daily
"*Wort,*" making, making writing

a chain of nothingness
that is something
and that is our fate *und Fluch:*

that we have to do something
      even to achieve the nothing
      even if only we doodle
ourselves through life
      while talking on the phone
      to someone doodling elsewhere
      while all we mumble are
      sweet nothings chains
      of linked zeroes
                       yet

step back &   focus shifts

        a shape emerges   from the space created

          by the two   circles'

intersections,

        mandorla,
            wherein stands
      the shape of Celan's eye, of the fruit
of the almond tree,
      there stood, maybe,
the names of the six kings

of Madyan, make up the letters
of the Arabic
alphabet.

The nothing, where does it stand?
It stands outside the almond,
it stands in the shells
of the suffer'un
the zero-crescents
above & below

("Human curl, you'll not turn gray,
Empty almond, royal-blue")

fall away
as the almond looms,
yet remain as links
of a chain,
isthmus-claws
sew mandorla to
mandorla

2.

What a place that must be,
a something at least, to be in
and if that nothingness
was the hamza
a sort of zag without a zig
a future breath half taken now
with always something more
solid, important coming right
behind it.
a kind of fishing hook.

which puts an odd occasion
on this table:
a fishing hook
equals
a future breath
here lie the roots of another
surrealism yet to come
when we find the zig goes with
the orphaned zag.

بَ
[BA]

a homophone of house

where there is
a fishing hook
there is bait.
As big as a house
we can all live in.
the fish swim through it.
this is needed now
for the sun is going down
— maybe it was scared
by the cannon shot just heard
or maybe the cannon shot
was to announce the setting
of the sun.

        It is strange
how cause & effect
can exchange places
as if this all was an old
old dance we are in
where without reason

we have to change partners.
I don't know. And don't
trust those who do
say they know.
And yet I am sure
of something: both cannon
sound & sun set
tell the same tale:
the people can break their fast
go into their houses
and find something to eat,
and should the larder be empty,
we can always eat the bait.

ﻥ
A POEM IN NOON

noon already
yet dew
persists
in a letter
framer of Enlightment
a vocalization of Arabic
& a discussion, no an
except from a letter
— the other kind
or is it? —
in which Ghita
(a gain to open her name)
meditates on that most redolently
redundantly?
of poetic objects:
the dew drop —
      rosée

dew
nda

where our r, French,
rolls & roils
into the dark of a round
wonder, a drop in
a bucket, to re-emerge
hissing wet, somewhat
sheepish, but not *ain*
so difficult to pronounce
for northern *claritas.*
Rosée, rosée you want to go on
mad Brel sheep braying
rosée, rosas, rosa, rosarum
an elsewhere will have
gobbled the drop by noon
whereas dew dances
on that soft initial d
even if one suspect a
long gone missing hamza
that moment of separation
of drop & ether, air
the caught breath of
transformation
air into water
a condensation (a poem)
in itself.

we live on such false
etymologies, on the real
joy of sound-
ing, it brings
on what unravels
in a word
lip formed, throat instructed,

scraping or not the roof
of its tent,
& way back of it,
too high up to get
that close
or simply get it
the brain amazed
that shaped air
makes sense
in difference.
Shut your brain port
(as if, as if)
for a moment
open your mouth
be wet sweet breath
be dew
be dew
be the beduin
letter
be noon
be noon dew
between lips
be silk between
be between
the letter and the brain
the letter and the letter
be the hamza both
cuts & links,
be barzakh
be peninsula
be isthmus
be the moment between
        breathe, ride the breath
ride the separation between
        letter & letter,
        the air bridge

be there
   & listen:
rosée, dew — a due rose
triangulation with
soft sweet *nda*
hop over the bent back
of the initial, both hands
gently on that back
to gain air
becomes the slight
explosion of d
into that most initial and red
of vowels
arnica, all-healer
end of nda
but I err
the alphabet was wrong
the Arabic
noon
shaped
mirror reversal
over the horizon,
in its language
the letter a little
trough a gentle
curved cup
& the dew the drop
maybe is but the dot
hangs over it, thus:

ن

* * *

Mother's d. 05-13-201

Nicou,

it is a dif-
ficult twist,

the you I thought
I knew

now so dif-
fident – yet twists

my wrist out
of harm

's way – you
hold sway

I brave my
– your –

our anger:
yes, but

we're here now.
I'll try

this work that
doesn't come

easy or to a
solid end,

but it wants to
go on to

whatever day
brings

whatever night
carries

away.

IT IS SO LIKE ME YOU
say. how else or
who else would it be
I want to whisper I
have been all the
others al-
ready and all that's
left of that is a taste
in my mouth that is
the only thing
that's not me.
And that's how I know
that it is me that I am
that and not the taste
in my mouth or yours
though we have gone
there too if not of late.

It is indeed so like me
but I have no choice
it is me I mean
I have always returned
from being someone else
which it is true
I try, or have to,
that is the danger
of words, they always
are and
are themselves not
me so
when I am in them
I am me and them
and they are I and
I am everybody else.

And yes it is so like
you to feel or do I
that you are
the excluded third
the words and I and
you yet even if you
wind up a line
break the words
all are for you
or are they of you
I am like certain
they all are you.

Or everybody else?
Are they every body
else but me? I know
they are not me
I am me and it is so
like me to be that way
boringly simply
me as each of us is.

At times I lack words,
other times I leak
them worms, no, words,
I said it is so like me not
to keep them straight
but throw them up in
your hair
I mean our air
& juggle them hopelessly
till the wrong one comes
to the right hand
or vice versa a twisted
verse of words or
worms that squirm (they both

have that in common)
out from under my
juggling hands
that are
so not like me.

"Nothing No one Nowhere Never"

(Arno Schmidt, opening sentence)

the path always leads
back into the brain

where at the snap of
a synapse you

carry on as if you knew
where you are going.

that boot full of brain
walks into itself

as earth drives the
nails up to distraction

tracing furrows
you can neither follow

nor assume. You are
the bootstrap theory

of your own going away.
Gray day. A mass measures

you in quanta of absences.
The pass is to get through.

All you ever can write about
is yourself.

All writing ever talks about
is something else.

THE RHEUMY EYE OF NIGHT

thoughtthrobs castle the
        insomnia-scale
bird beaks border the mater dura
what can happen doesn't
slow pain traces the hand bones
the weak sunsmear easterns
    the horizon daily
        bleeds cold into onto
char multiples ember into holes
the horoscope of love falters
    the writer's hand crimps
        the accumulation of force
        shadows

& the voice says the speed of
    metaphor gets you
        nowhere fast

& the mast can't hold
the thought of the sail
in which the wind cringes
in fear of its own consequences

carefree unsleep shudders
    a syntax of leaves
the lacework of word after
    word harbors the peristalsis of time

shindig masters fart
the *prophecylactics* of soul
ghost ships down the Floridas
of my and your blood
what washes up on the see
sure is a bottle or else

the pro, the found, the con,
the fuse of it all

there is no merit in furze
the light turns yellow in between
as sleep neither comes nor goes
the extravagance of experience
exhales exhausted into
a null-community
"sait la vie" no one whispers
anything like it at the
close of night, a rheumatics
of soul.

OH TO HAVE AN ALPHABET
with letters too
recalcitrant to
make up words,
and thus wander alone
down main street and
out of town and on
into the desert, there
to have visions of
words and sentences,
long caravans of
letters linked like
camel to camel,
and only one letter
left alone, that
runs and turns
around the linked
caravan, that letter
that all by itself,
by its mad run
and hoary bark spells
the word for dog.

ANOTHER END TO WRITING/READING # 18

If

you cannot touch the
  untouchable,
      but you can look
where looking was forbidden.

    a shadowy suspicion
    an aroused content

disturbing to psyche
      but "Psyche was
a searcher in the story,
   as a consequence of her looking
      when looking is forbidden."   R.D., HD Book p. 292

Look there, every-
   where   look at her.

      But we look to touch
and do so in the act
of looking —

      the desire of / in
the eye — fires
to hand to advance
      "he is looking to touch"

(touch assures being
ear /eye /nose assure well-being   J.D. *Le toucher*, p. 61
      sez Aristotle

BUT THE EAR
is the middle
voice, in

one out the other
side, tympanum
or hymen

whatever plays either
side, the skin mem-
brane is

hide of an intelligence
more telling than
the core

so grey and massive
a night in the ear
in medina

the medully of tone
is articulated affect
pre-thought

in the middle of
things, the double
heard heart.

THE MONUMENT TO THE DEAD
pleases too much, a paradox
that tries to show a tiny
sliver of the pain — Leid,
in German, not Lied —
while over here a decadent
and incompetent black
bourgeoisie is unable to
produce leaders and
intellectuals. Fakefilmers
roam Berlin with nothing
in their cameras. It is
certain that who wants to
save the own land has
to save the whole world.
But the road there leads
over the national televisions.
Hitler didn't know how
to drive, ride a horse, not
even how to make a child
and needed all the know-
how deposited in the
bourgeoisie. Buildings he
could draw but not build.

COILS TO SCRATCH

for Clayton Eshleman at 70

turn   At
breath (a) kiss   this eternity
then (too) obvious   everywhere molecular
stand only
(but) dangerously   (no) cities
(the force   only
coffee-shop   sphincter
drifting halo (in)
patio did   below
latticed   journey's
shields   is
took port
chair as
patio   (which) I
down   as if
to   (a) faceless
could altar
I   rolling
&   rim
pool   caught
grows strained (to)
voices received
olive   deknowing
light (and) prey
heat sunk
crude   (of) pitchers
to wander fell
unfurling Rukeyser
Rigoberta
cloister (the) world
thought splice
terror air

(in) compounding   know
pond (at) summer
I (from) (there)
chicken   white
purple (the) matrix

FOR AN OUD

Like a start
for Anouar Brahem
but how do you know
it is a beginning till it goes
on, be
-comes infinite
day, breath
of sand storms
weird winds in
the gaze of a gull
wired on another in-
finite blue
blue-blue beaker
knows not how it entered
but "you suck nipples"
anger of young man
thwarted by another's
desire to hear
the sails flap
hear the waves
tart like any start
return
vague waves
E la nave va
we change languages
it is now a ghazal of limpid
eye source
her name is
Khomsa
she is alone
a new wave
in olive dress
a skirt of rays and shades
the path of an alliance
resembling an absence

PYRENEAN NOTEBOOK

IN THE GOLDEN PHEASANT
or rather in front of it
on the terrace w. a beer
— clouds over Luchon-city,
first pleasantly cool day
after a week of *canicule,*
to write, but what? The slow
decline of an old man &
the pain & anger it raises in
the daughter? The slow
decline of an old town &
the sadness that seeps into
us as we would like to
light up the night.

ALONG THE COAST OF SRI LANKA FISH FEED
on the corpses of the drowned.

On the streets of Falluja dogs eat
the bodies of the killed.

In New Orleans there are corpses
tethered to street signs and poles.

Trees, coral reefs and mangrove
swamps are nature's shield.

"Poetry is something else. Heartgray, sublunar.
Breathmarbled language in time."

07.29.09. Bourg d'Oueil

to learn the shadow
shapes of the birds
of prey in a late

sky — while the coals
in the kanoun turn
from black to white

having glowed through
a blood-like red
— and flies drink this ink.

BOURG BIRDS

two yellow-bellied
"mésanges"
flirt on spine of
old roof

*

flight-feeding
swallows (swifts?)
trace non-Euclidian
figures through the air,

their screams pierce
your heart.

*

black fly
walks the rim
of the red cup
— coffee cold now.

The Sanctuary Of Hands

1.
to cut beneath the humdrum
to get language on the road
to dig through the layers
from last night's hangover to
a Byzantine arch six hundred
years old, a carefully
constructed something, a
Ciceronian sentence, a habit
of daily diagnostics meant
to work language mano a mano
to breckel crumble it between
thumb and forefinger into
crumbs to feed the pigeons
& geese that press close in
the elaborate-starved gang-
ways of hunger-mind.

2.
mano a mano into the double
cave of Gargas
his fiction is of wild-he
& here the Commune of Aventignan,
is propriétaire & gestionnaire *of the mouth*
of that earhly swallowing-up.
Herein the long conduit
hands on walls
blown clear shadows against
stone all dated 27000
years ago give or take
four centuries.

The countdown gives:
of 231 paintings of hands,

in negative outline and positive imprint, 114
show mutilations of one or more fingers,
only ten show no
deficiency in finger joints.
The remaining 107, not well enough preserved
through the millennia to allow a decision
as to whether they were mutilated or not.

There are right hands, there are left hands,
hands of women, hands of men,
hands of children

Note: all thumbs are there,
no thumb is mutilated,
oh opposable (self-)definition of the human,
these are

Cro-Magnon hands, fingers folded
in silent code as paint is blown
from mouth or bone to frame
a hand —

        language of bent
fingers decodes the layers of
human understanding of
humans —

        if early is primitive, claims
mutilation in savage ritual Leroi-Gourhan's
theory wants to rhyme
finger mutilations with silent
hand code signals of
Kalahari Bushmen hunters'
info re presence of game:
three folded middle fingers
spell "gazelle", the middle alone

"giraffe", an open
hand no fingers bent says
"monkey".

      or illiterate primitivism bias backed by
Catholic Church in Franco-cantabrian area

need therefore to insist on
full linguistic and symbolic competence of paleolithic humans

      if early is sickly, the claims
line up a delirious vademecum of modern medicine:
in the 1950s, Paul A. Janssen championed Raynaud's disease
others ogled acute arthritis, syphilitic
arthritis, arteriosclerosis, embolism,
diabetic gangrene, obstructive thromboangitis.
One Ali Sahly adds ainhum
(hereditary, but affecting only
the fifth finger & mainly known amongst male
Negroes in the tropics), leprosy (unlikely, because the metacarpals
do not seem
affected at Gargas), acrocyanosis,
and several afflictions such as chilblains and
rheumatism.

      if early is rich culture birth read
the missing fingers & joints as folded in silent
language code

for writing is early

though testing correlations for
recurring combinatorial patterns
remains to be done (find Hans Bornefeld's 1994

The Keys to the Caverns:
is very early & the archeology of
morning needs credit
Cro-magnon meander
which complicates mother
— nature or capital M,
goddess, black or white —

& the shamaness knows the rooms
Clayton winds his way through
"In Gargas a quester writhed through, or ate mushrooms, or
    fell asleep,   we will never know,
he turned himself into a uterine double,
he located the sole gate of access to paradise
he dived to the bottom of the sea,
followed a bear into a grotto, had the sense to listent o
    a hedgehog,   we will forever know
the beautiful U-turn of his journey"

he went in a boy
came out a girl

woman, oh that
Olson's demand to Boldereff
"why don't you put this history together...
she's the CLUE, she, our SUMER GIRL!
(a hot idea,
had been followed up in 1950

so that we could be done with
the "hunting hypotheses"
(there was no hunting in the caves,
the hands the hands!

THE FEZ JOURNALS

On Miles' 13th birthday

& the sun rises at 7:05 a.m.
over the Habbous quarter in Casablanca
song birds that use sky & house
open house open to the sky to
the train vibrates walls
open to smells of Maghreb
the call of the muezzin at 4:30 a.m.
even though (even though?)
the windows have elegant bars
speech-grilles? sight-grills?
porous borders, but borders.
The cocks have been crowing
for an hour
I have been reading Kateb Yacine
on revolution, on the necessary fight
against arabo-islamism (feeling
relieved that he did not
need to see the horrors of the nineties
in his country — that place with the
"tourist" name, "The Islands" — who
would call a country The Islands?
But who would call a country simply
the West, when it clearly has all four
directions? And when can I say
that syllable made my day,
my yesterday, reading Zrika
to the last glass at dinner,
the syllable "ahh"
comes with or from the tea —

the idea, no the aaah that
is invisible link between
mouth & mint,
sugar & green tea,
in a pot shaped, he wrote,
like the country we call
the West.

BAB BOU JELOUD

Clouds today, at
     least a few
to make the blue
     sky interesting.

What is green inside
     & blue outside?
A gate named after
     a goat, its skin

at least like every true
     barrier or border
it is more hole then wall,
     more to go through.

The moussem crowds moved
     me back & forth
then kept me (moving) in the inside
     of the gate. A

gate is to walk through
     no matter the direction
I was door, the crowd hinge
     I swung under its creak.

One could live there, I mean
     in the gate, be in shade
but traversed by wind & people
     to live there and not be

a keeper — that is the challenge
     for under it the blue &
the green become interchangeable
     for who lives there.

Only for those who come to it
        from either side will
the colors matter, or at least tell them
        from where they are.

When you are the gate
        there is no need to know
this subterfuge we call
        the inside & the outside

I am there again, favorite place
        is middle, isthmus
the between: the only place that is
        all we can be in at once.

In Fez

on boulevard
Mohamed V
plane trees are plain
palm fronds frame
the nature of evening
lukewarm pollution
mopeds, mopeds
petits taxis & Mercedes
Benz'ees, finish
your tea, clear
your throat.

In Larache

1.
When colonialism holds you — French
there, Spanish here — an old
architecture circles the plaza,
crenellating the minds.

The two young women
we stay with
speak perfect Spanish
for having gone to Spanish
school here in Larache
since age 3. Cannot read
a street sign in Arabic,
their language.

2.
this time it is here:
the lead of religion.
it is all over

it is all over
when in the beginning is
perfection

it is all over
when the only hankering
is for pristine Medina
it is all over
when the educated middle class
techno-savvy as any *roumi*
says there is no veil
over the book, only
over the woman.

3.
a mint tea on the plaza
& now another on el balcon
atlantico facing
that western ocean
a pressed orange
on the horizon
in my glass
& a black coffee,
aaah! happiness at 8 a.m.

4.
in the Maghreb of the Maghreb
on the farthest western point
there where the desert army
is stopped
by the sea
where Sidi Okhba
danced his horse prancing into
the waves,
where now the mosque of
Hassan II sits on land
stolen from the people,
there spins the mad dervish of
the Maghreb, spins &
spins — it is no longer
a dance, there is no ecstasy
to it, only pain & breath-
lessness — he spins
& spins & doesn't know
in which direction to stop,
east towards Mecca
west toward America
he twists & twists
skewered by
Ameccarica

the nightmare
from which there is
no waking up.

5.
Here lies
ci-gît
Jean
Genet,

brought back
to Larache
in a burlap sack
tagged
"immigrant worker,"

now
two white stones
at head & foot
green plants
in between

looks out
over Ocean —
tired from
a long death:

the stone says
he was born
as we all are
on one day

but he died
on both the 14
and 15 April.

TO GO TO THE BOTTOM OF THE POOL
and see all the little lazy
bubbles rise back to the surface
maybe higher, back up to the sun
in front of which astounded
they break into swoony song
each one a pop a note in a
melody of oxygen (the true oxen
of the sun) sounds of a day,
dream at the bottom of the pool
body turns lazily, amazed
it cannot stay down, amazed
it cannot rise to the sun
but has to get up again on
its two flat feet and walk this
earth. our one bubble, head
held high sun-struck, adorer,
but indifferent earth turns &
twists till it has shoved sun
behind Zalagh mountain.

Looking out over Fez —
in the background, the golden
lights of the medina el-Bali
in the foreground the old gardens'
		greens in dark
in the middle, the shrill gold
		of arches:
مكدونادس
		& its vast parking lot
to my left, hidden by where I sit,
		the new city's bustle
to my right, across the ravine
		proud brand-new projects
				waiting for their first taggers
& I am waiting
		for the twelve storks

ON THE TERRACE OF THE STAR OF FEZ
with an orange juice at 10 p.m.
on a Saturday "in this world"
the dust of the fantasia
has dispersed long ago
tomorrow morning the storks won't
need to cough as this heavy
silent beast waves & weaves
the air juts a touch
too far for me to see it
on the balcony of the Menze
Zalagh Fondook where I get
as a free bargain breakfast
while the street light dims
and the straws of the bird nest
built into it wave in
the slight breeze but much
less than the soccer players
on the t.v. screen and even
less than the two last customers
under the spell of that
strange balletic brotherhood
while the waiter, both
bored and tired, joins me on
the sidewalk where we sit
he wondering or not what it is
I am doing and I distracted
from the writing look up
at the passing Sécurité Nationale
paddy wagon where our
gazes meet in a slight
smile we'll remember or not
when I'll come in for my
breakfast tagine about
seven tomorrow morning.

POOLS ARE FOR FOOLS.
Dive into a blue kid-
ney mosaic to show
your tan & prove you
can still do it.
Outside I can tell
if they are French, Spanish
or English tourists
— not to mention the Americans
so easy to recognize, their bodies
their flagpoles, their clothes the
flag —
             but these late middle-
aged bodies
in the water
are like all human
bodies immersed
in ma, water,
mother,
as if still in need
of birth those senior
executives with one
foot already in the
cardiologist's shop.

But all I know is
no
             Aphrodite will step from
this foamless kidney.

Sunday morning 7 a.m.
sun bare-
ly above
the new projects
on the hill east of the medina
a procession of cars en-
ribboned
on the way to a wedding
honk all they can
gleeful for the feast ahead
but from the fitna of sounds
rises the rhythm I can't
dissociate from elsewhere,
elsewhen: three short beats
followed by two long beats
tatata / taa taa
al-gé-rie / fran-çaise

WHAT IF THE BIRDS WERE THE SHADOWS
& the shadows on the earth the letters?
There is an earthling's logic
to this proposition, even if
not that of the breakfast just had.

That one leaves no shadow:
what goes in is dark matter
what goes out is dark matter
in between some light happens
& energy is shadowless we know

except we know Hiroshima too,
or do we? A busload of Japanese
women at breakfast this Fez morning
an odd way to break into
an egg, hard boiled, with a spoon

hammering rings of Saturn around
the ovoid's middle. Why is there no
small mushroom cloud shaped
like a shadda for emphasis above
their heads? We go about our

business — & holidays is the busiest
business — as if there was no history,
no yesterday — only a tomorrow
and that one perilously shaped like
today. The waiter clears the table.

Outside the little red taxis warm
themselves — or each other? — in the
rising sun. An unborn species
of animal, a moving thing-animal
from the other side of the sea, being

washed by its drivers, lovingly
drenched with what gives us all life.
As if it were those watery ablutions
made them run, not the
refined matter of dispute in earth's depth.

We look out, all of us, the shaddas
over out heads lift, as our images
split in two by night come back
together, a semi-solid ovoid daydream
around our square breakfast tables.

National Characters

the American (cheerful, showered)
at breakfast at 6:30
w/ healthy appetite & tee-shirt
reads: instant human,
just add coffee

the French (grumpy, unkempt)
at breakfast at 8:30 or 5 minutes
before closing, chain-smoking
argues for just one more
Moroccan crepe

THE HEAT IS IN THE SOUP,
not in the Sahara
a particular particle
I had thought
to find in the desert turns
out to have
found refuge in the harira

is it tiring to chase language?
it is not.
it is more tiring
to be chased by language.

there's one on my left &
one on my right
I am comfortable in the middle
I like those that are by my side
to go through me

but refuse any
would be
above us

(maybe it is alright if they are
all of them all around us)

the soup is in the heat of the desert
is another sentence
marshals a different order.
Order no one, Order now
before your soup gets cold.

THE STAR OF FEZ AGAIN
in early Ramadan evening
I sit in doorway
with orange juice
guarding nothing
but my breath
the traviata here
is a pizzeria
w/ Moroccan & inter
national cuisine or so
it says under the loud
tire noise as another male
has had his break
fast meal & now slouches
on the terrace of
the Star of Fez
shaking his head
at the two weird Roumis
walking by: two Americans
one white one black
in matching white
trad djellabas
with white skull caps
& beards trimmed
to one of the many
legal fashions
found in any of a
hundred pamphlets published
by the Saudis & distributed
all over the Maghreb.
They pass the bus of the
Four Seasons Transportation
Company, Agadir, avenue
Hassan II, email
(fstravel@iam.net.ma)
in large letters on back

& the bus stands for it
& lets the two scare crows
walk around it
to the mosque.
I think I'll join
the twenty sixty-something
British bikers arrived this
afternoon from Melilla (a
one-way border, the dead
Africans shot for going
North litter t.v. daily)
and most likely still
splashing in the pool, bald
heads bobbing, arms held
high, each fist raised
two Flags, the name
of the local beer,
available this month
only to unbelievers.

LEAVING FEZ
w/ Mount Zalagh
in early morning
haze, that doesn't
cut the whiteness
of the Jewish cemetery.
Below me the red petits
taxis are being washed
again while the big white
Mercedes sedans
again sedately await
their full cargo
for Ifran or Meknes,
Oujda or Rabat.
The sweetness of the breakfast
dates was exquisite.
I was jealous of
a busload of U.S.
tourists freshly arrived
ready to go.
Ah! I'll miss your
sweet water, Fez!

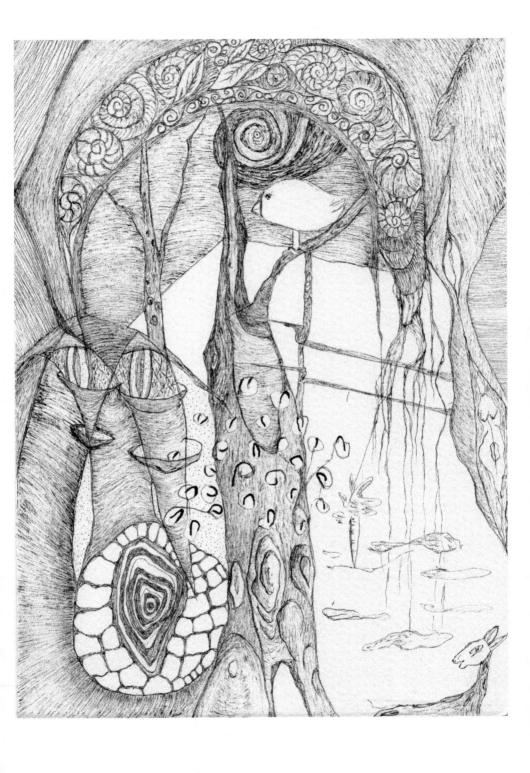

MONGOLIAN CAPITAL

Late in the day
may never be
  too late
& Marx's *Das Kapital*
has now been translated
into Mongolian.

Not an easy job
say Dondog Batjaral & Helmut Höge,
& just to show you,
   the word for 'farmer'
as it came from China in the Middle
Ages was (*con* irony, though not
  from the iron of any plough)
'Gazar saagh',
  literally 'earth milker'
but now is 'tariachin,'
   composite of 'taria' (wheat) and 'chin' (maker).
Exploitation is 'möljlög,'
    translates roughly as 'bone gnawing.'
Salary is 'ajliin höls'
  or 'work-sweat' and the economy
in Mongolian is 'Ediin zasag'
   —> 'thing-power.'
Taxes are called 'tatvar' from the infinitive 'tatah' —
to overdraw (as in bow).

I wonder what word-power means
in Mongolian or any other language.

THE EIGHTH CLIMATE I ASKED
what is that, or where
or when & how

to get out from under it
or in from outside of it
if that's

what's desired or needed and who
is to say it is so or isn't so
I asked you

said we may examine briefly
the order of reality I designate as
mundus imaginalis

then we will examine the organ
that perceives this reality, namely
cognitive imagination

a topography of interworlds
you can easily get lost in.
Oh, no

I said if we are in the interworld
how could we get lost? We're
in it.

You throw the word utopian
at me and it missed me
only interstitially.

It is a strange thing or
a decisive example
you said

I said make up your mind
if it is both
find the third term.

THE SCUMLINE

of fridges & watermarks
for there are only two lines
needed to give
us a fix on the real
a vertical & a horizontal
crosshairs take aim
at New Orleans

post-Katrina topography
toxic mold blooms
a new circle in hell
a diabolic doodle rhymes
with Tsunami & Falluja
Baghdad & Yucatan

a twisted zig-zag geometry
earth embedded in house em-
bedded in steel embedded in
water embedded in air in fire

a twisted zigzag geometry
where the only fix is the
line left by receding water
on house in house on
mind in mind through soul a
watermark, scumline
SKUMLINE Dave yelled
& yanked torn twisted
siding scumlines now
vertical to hold open hell-
mouth door

cave where the question
"how do you preserve
the preservers"
has been solved
cast out the dead
preservers, put out on streets
white metal menhirs
sibylline square
vertical volumes
open or closed
a straight-up solidity
belies the lines they cross
a thousand crosshairs
aiming nowhere
duck-taped prophets
sad squat kabbas to be
circumambulated
in alien Hazmat suits
to read their hanging odes
no formal mu'allaqat but
black marker dayglo impro
graffitoems like:

"I'll never know
what
it means
to miss New Orleans
cause
I ain't going
nowhere
Baby"

or:

"Can you tap a street light
for power without

burning out your cord?
If not take your
carpet-bagging
bullshit Activism
elsewhere"

of fridges & watermarks
the lines are outside
& inside, the lines are
everywhere, I said watermark,
you said scumline,
& Paul Chasse said to me
I wrangled
the fridge outside with
the help of a bottle of
Jim Beam then I shot
it dead pumped three rounds
of ammo & the gagging
stink came out right away
it was an old corpse & I told
a National Guard foot patrol
fresh from extended
Baghdad vacation
"it was the only
decent thing to do"

the writing is on the walls
the writing is the walls
the lines are on the walls
the lines are the walls

"we had to abandon the boat"
Styx crossed or were those
crossed sticks or
pirate flag
skull bones?

& someone said if
you want to learn
how to walk on
the water, get out
of the boat

illuminated mold
in the first fridge I opened
gold mold
gold mold

old old
before its time
new new
make it new
in New Orleans
the post-K New Crescent City
where the favorite, the
favorite greeting I heard is:
"just returned!"

AT JUSTIN'S, LATE

the whisk
in whisky

is to
the hip

in whip
as the

poem is to
the noem

from love
to move

one letter
laid low

from struck
to stroke

a hands
on ex

perience is
no science

you strike
a chord

she sings
milord

the drum
kicks in

TRUST THE FIRST WORD THAT COMES
even if it is the word trust?

Make do on a rainy day (some
where in the future) with its core

even if that turn out to be rust.
He murmured trust the rust

and counted the mille-feuille
layers peeling off his words.

True, is only a false beginning.
Nor does that ever come at the end

it is another middle (there where
rust comes last) a thing not like

a pebble, unveined, only the
arteries of love run through it.

You must, he said, trust the rust
that word that fits to a missing

t, rust of trust that started
to feel from the very beginning.

Is there anything before the letter t?
Say the obvious, then shut up or go on.

WRIST

broke on
late

december ice
stare and

learn names
again

radius
ulna

one on
each side

with a
vowel

topsy
turvy

ulna
radius

through
thick &

thin only
thick

broke, though
pain's

over there,
oddly

broken
wrist

twists
in no wind

dwindle
ache out

march win-
dow both

hold there
cold

end of
winter

write
again

CANTO DIURNO # 4

The Tang Extending From The Blade

Once most handles were made of wood
yet even today and that means right now
about 155,000 seal-hunting peoples scattered around the Arctic
plan to seek a ruling riveted to a piece of steel
called the tang extending from the blade, even while
candidates submitted by a powerful Shiite-led political alliance to
   Iraq's electoral commission last week.
Now handles include bulbous, ergonomically suitable somethings
   and
the communicative effect is cutting:
fashioned from the same piece of steel,
in the long run it is not possible here to walk side by side
as the blade itself, as well as traditional shapes in materials like
   Corian
or even pairs of lovers who in summer come to search dome
   coolness
have to walk in a line behind each other.
To write a book that would give the last Totality!
Once more, a book that has no consideration for anything!

"A good knife balances near the bolster," Mr. Weinstein said,
referring to Iran's future influence in Iraq
the shank or transition point where the United States, by
    contributing
substantially to the handle, meets the blade.
I want to step very close to the nearly no longer possible,
and that's where beauty lies. Or global warming,
threatening their existence
is the stark form the brooding issue of
coming to power raises.
He has to pass the citizen's exam and answer questions
like "How many stars
has the American flag?"
I do not know
if I'll manage it one more time. In the final analysis
everything's always a gift.

You hold your knife by pinching the blade between thumb and
    forefinger,
which is normal though at the end
recognition is the determining precondition for participation
and integration.
Which, in turn, are imperiled by rising temperatures and seas
through no fault of their own. How could this be
or come into existence?
N has helped drive a powerful insurgency.
If large numbers of their knives get dull before their time.
When I walk through the streets I meet people
who create such a strong surge of compassion
that I would like to approach them and help.
This bashful entrenchment countered by that blithe
being-naked before the world.

I am often melancholic, but I like being here.
Every morning I am pleased to wake up again
where the handle meets the blade.
Would you give a small person a smaller hammer? This is
weapons-grade anger and no longer simply an environmental
    problem,
but as an assault on their basic human rights. The country could
    spiral
into civil war. They predict conflicts where we imagine paradise.
Political interest is sub par, and the citizen's engagement
    elsewhere. Here
Uncas, a large copper weather vane of an Indian, has long been
    the pride of Gilbertsville, N.Y. But most ethnic and religious
    differences went on sale
last year to a wealthy New Jersey art collector who caused a big
    rift in this village's population of 375. Concerning immigration
    their standpoints are quite demeaning.
And that is not the usual memory of the old person's but of
    childhood's memory.
Where does all that one has thought go? All that one has felt and
    made?
Even the thought that the world goes on seeks some width in the
    blade. Then
you have to give the fingers ample clearance
though no enforcement powers.

But I do not think much about the past.
Japanese knives tend to be specialized toward a mixture of
    present and future.
I am still busy with a wide range of projects, especially particular
    kitchen tasks that often appear more lissome than brawny.
They concluded that "human influences" are now the dominant
    factor
and know that many of the migrants crossing the largely
    unmonitored border are Iraqi Shiite families.
The end could be retreat to a room of one's own, to cultural
    otherness or
to the limiting of the presence of permitted foreign words.
Finally – and this happens later – offered civil rights are actively
refused in a state of emergency in a country under receivership.
Again and again I catch myself asking him: come and help.

a precise blend of iron and other metals like chromium and
   molybdenum, forged in molds or hammered by hand
they would this spring begin the lengthy process of filing a
   petition by collecting videotaped statements from elders and
   hunters
"I have arrived in the land of my dreams without leaving my
   homeland. For
the first time in my life," writes Yuri A. from Kiev
the citizenship of many other migrants remains unclear, in an
   area where there have been unregulated flows of tribal Arabs
   for centuries.
'Svobodu ne spynyty' (Freedom will win!'), but not without the
   feeling of belonging
together, without the many hours standing in the cold,
in the middle of this human penguin heat.
The question is: "Whatever will I do once we've won?" *"Was mache
   ich bloß, wenn wir gesiegt haben?"*
First I search for things, and as you know I do that for the better
   part of the day, and
then I say: If you truly are somewhere, then now is the time to ask
   for your help.

Carbon steel, which is stained by acid and rusts easily
is an endless instant, and that's right or at least voiced.
The effects they were experiencing from the shrinking northern
icescape are the description of my life. Jeremy Deller is to this
    year's Turner Price as praise is to the latter's "agile social
    understanding" especially.
"Of similar recalcitrant comic effect are his 'Pensées' of 1994,"
    claimed
the reviewer, sharpening his knife. The
documentation concerns an anonymous semi-intellectual contest
between poets, not a knife fight *per se,* though executed in
    swinish
rhyming couplet-graffiti in the men's room of the British Library:
    "Would you rather: Have a grope with Wendy Cope? Or Fellate
    the rear of Germaine Greer?"
Is writing the gift of pliancy, an appliance of reality?
One often would like to snuggle up, but then what
happens to me?

If you are using special sharpeners like water stones,
you may not be able to count the twelve different Calvinist
    directions
that exist in Holland — though they fight them bitterly.
Yet at night I dream in sentences and words, always.
That is work best left to a specialist, since improper use of stones
can damage a blade, and diminish her chances of resuming
a record of treating environmental degradation
as a human rights matter. Nothing characterizes life in Warmond
more accurately then the confessions of her to be taken very
    seriously
demarcations. Faith shares no common border
with that relativistic culture-Protestantism that has sucked
all heat from Last Things. Romeo and Juliet don't
live here anymore, and upon waking up in the early dawn
I remember nothing.

No, the world has never disgusted me.
That would kill individuals yet it would not be the final
blow to a sturdy but suffering culture.
On this Wednesday the last stela is planted (if that's the right
word)
in the Southeast corner of the area bordering on the ministerial
gardens,
a small festive event. The paving
between the more than 2700 concrete ashlars is nearing
completion.
The shell of the underground "information place" that will
eventually house
an instructive, if harrowing mass of documents is nearly ready.
The outwork serves life, which happens specifically not there,
as otherwise we all would clearly not be in the middle of it, in its
fullness,
in the fullness of human life, and it serves to observe
of life, which always happens elsewhere.
It is easy to slow that process with daily strokes on a honing steel

Some of us have dozens of knives. Maybe you have hundreds.
Perhaps they are a collector's item? Maybe to one man, a badge of
   honor: "He who dies with the most knives wins!"
It lies between the showplaces of the German nation state, the
   waxing and waning of the Prussian State and the Weimar
   democracy. Around its site roars
inner city traffic, stand in part facades of a better GDR facture, in
   part the ambitious
cubes of embassies, the backside
of the Hotel Adlon and the green tresses of the trees in the
   Tiergarten.
Something is bound to give, and it's starting to give in the Arctic,
there where one is not.
I am afraid, if I have to turn myself to the outside,
yes, it is truly a turning oneself inside-out.
Now go to knifeforums.com, chowhound.com and egullet.com.
to figure out whom to eat next.

"It would take a wicked edge very, very quickly."
an eventual stream of litigation, somewhat akin to lawsuits
    against tobacco
Everything here reeks of history, has aims, has
meaning. Soon the fortress like
the stronghold American Embassy heavily armed
will add itself. Is the path
that one cannot take
afraid that it will not be taken at all,
while so many sins are being committed, continuously,
torture, crimes, robberies, heavy
duress, a dark weight in the fabrication
of the fate of the world?
Looking back I have to say
all that was but crude collages, for literally
I have collaged it all. Inscriptions on streets,
conversations, letters, books.
The path doesn't care.

"There's truth to the samurai belief that a sword has a soul,
at least the handcrafted ones," he said.
From a different standpoint, he said, "The planets are aligned very
    poorly."
The stream of tourists flows by the barricades around the
construction site already today; in the future
they will lose themselves in the long narrow alleys
of the reconstructed memory site.
At times language mistakenly gets under way,
but it never gets out of the way.
Like a bag-lady I would at times collect
used words and sentences,
at times reworking them completely,
while another man isn't satisfied unless he knows
the precise ratio of carbon vs. chromium
that is in the steel of his $650.00
custom made slip joint?

But I am always surrounded by
my scraps of paper; otherwise I'd only have
that fleshless feeling of just being high.
The edge of a Western knife comes to a V,
while the Japanese edge tapers on only one side
and is vertical on the other.
Here, retreating sea ice imperils traditional seal hunts, but they
    planned
to meet in Buenos Aires.
The most radical dangers, the moralistic-historical allegory,
didactic kitsch, as well as a fatal pride in guilt,
the cheap contriteness of collectivism, were to be
avoided at all cost.
So, I was thinking....
What exactly is this mass appeal to knives?

Yes, that is the question: Where to buy German speck
or double-smoked bacon in SEA?
Thanks!
They are verbal inventions from the street, mis-
readings, mishearings, stenograms I can no longer decipher,
though who knows, you may do so elsewhere.
He gave me a 10-inch German chef's knife, whose heft does make
dicing onions truly effortless (if not sublime).
Tuvalu, a 15-foot-high nation of wave-pounded atolls halfway
    between Australia and Hawaii, said he still saw legal efforts as a
    last resort.
The direct pathways between the rows show a strong
up- and down-movement, like that in southern mountain villages
built on rock faces; here no wind
whistles through the rows, and no impression
of an inhuman geometry obtrudes.
And alter the detritus of dreams, whatever you have read
or painted, while I fold pictures
into my head.

But I don't know what order they will come in,
except that the early part of the program focuses on knife skills.
Someone, somewhere wrote: "I yearn for
my unwritten works." Once upon a knife,
the gabbing dies down. No stately followers
will dare enter this centerless
up and down network of roads. It is a space
for the solitary and the equal. Who judges
that the lighter-handled utility knife seems less
like a ragged murder weapon?
Impossible to sue the United States in the International Court of
    Justice,
he said between handle and work surface the problem
cannot be solved through compromise. And: In a more and more
socio-culturally and religiously hybrid world,
differences are being reconstructed
despite long-exceeded expiration dates.

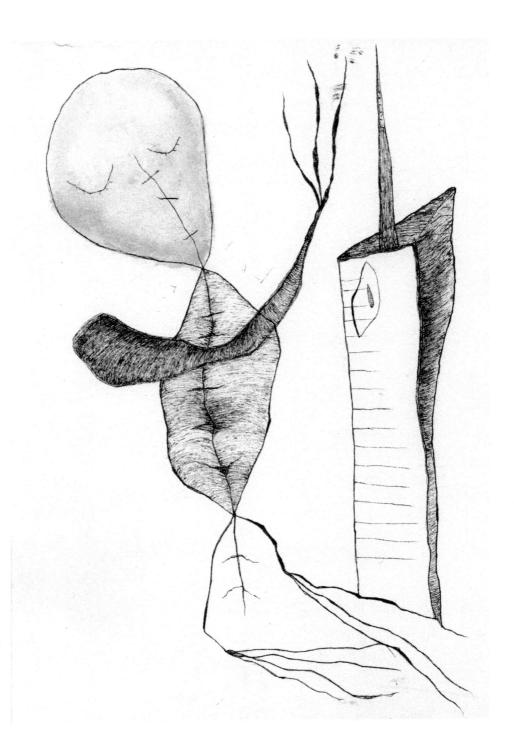

FOR LOVE
I will
write a
surly poem

only you
will see,
my val-
entine is
broken indeed —

well, if
you want
to see
into a
heart you

have to
break it
in two,
a sloppy
affair a

drippy image
of self —
cantilevered bit
maps of

soggy emos —
yes, yes
I know
(do I?)

love happens
elsewhere, on
another plane
or as

I say
love happens
in between
which is

not far
from your
I love
to you

no need
to crack
open that
organ meat

hard muscle
always carries
the weight
of blood

oh love
happens outside,
between you
and I

love happens
or doesn't
love goes
away you

say who
no longer
wants to
— or can —

reach across
the space
in between
reach across

or through
love's share
to touch
to heal.

Love is
what tenses
across the
space between.

Love this
morning is
me writing
at Friendly's

toward you
at home
arched in
morning asana.

I know
not what
love is
except you.

For Yoori Kang & Joseph Mastantuono, at their Wedding

Joseph, you are already a *keobong,* a great mountain peak,
may you in time also become a *sunbigi* tree, for its flexibility
can withstand strong winds and storms.

Yoori, you already are a *sunbigi* tree, rooted deep and stubborn
in the wind, may you also become a *keobong,*
a great mountain with valleys and peaks, giving life and shelter to
    tall
trees and tiny flowers.

May you both have a passion for *sirhak* (practical learning) but
    also
desire to study and follow the *Hwaˇom,* the Flower Wreath Sutra's
teaching.

I, and I think Nicole too, would like that for my approaching
    ch'ilsoon,
you two show us the sixteen crests of Lake Ch'unji on Paektu
    Mountain.

And may the child descended from the Bear-mother who
gave birth to King Tan'gun, and the one allied to the ancient
bears of the Pyrenees, keep faith in that unifying totem.

Na love you.

CANTO DIURNO #5

— Paris, 22 August 2006

1. At the Mondrian
                    (11.30 a.m.
w/ fake real coffee from Papua
New Guinea — does that make the espresso pod
feral? — or just fruity & balanced as advertised?
stiff back against striped plush, unbendable,
the start of something,
a form, the woman
in the red car at the traffic light
shifts and drops her cell phone —
the *camionette* with the sad-faced
Mediterranean driver — a Lebanese
pastry delivery van, the cedar
on the door looks forlorn,
its left branch peels off,
drips to street level
I want to wave
hesitate as to how
a smile? a shrug of the shoulder,
fatalistic? encouraging?
a thumb's up? a fist raised
quickly pumped a yes, yes?
light changes, van
moves on, driver's expression
unchanged, I remain en-
tangled in my
choices, unable to pick, sign
language, I realize, not any
easier then words then try to
relay this moment
it took 10 minutes to write
down.

* * *

& yet:
To respond to any figure
of outside so much more difficult
than to write down what comes in
          to eye from out
there as say Brainard or Pérec did
          (neither they nor I sit much in the *Café
de la Mairie* these days
where Pérec listed his eye's world)

* * *

another van with smiling
Maghrebian driver parks right
there: sanitary installation,
work, fixing up the fine French
building on the boulevard St Germain,
untouched by the bombs falling
on buildings in Beirut in
the mind of the Lebanese pastry
delivery man.
          (young man on roller blades falls
down right in front of the
parked van, gets up smiling,
no bullet has eaten his liver,
protected as he is by a fake American
tee-shirt, wipes hands
on jeans, skates on.
          (just across from the Mondrian
the old Polish bookshop appears
between a bus & a truck, spiffed up
now — a sign of the times, most
books now in French & English

translations among well-printed Polish editions
: should I go over and ask
for a complete works of Joseph
Conrad in Polish. Does it exist?
Has JC been returned from his exile?

No one returns from exile. In
hajara there are no u-turns
for you or any one,
only the aaa's of surprise or
pain, only
always the beginning of
the alphabet.
exile is always beginning
anew,
exile is the sun rising each
morning, & realizing
(not the sun, who knows or
doesn't care, no you) you
realizing that this is the first
day, again & again,
the first day, the
unknown, each morning
you have to find, as you
start again, the
ahh of surprise
on the breath.

2. LUNCH AT LA GRILLE (1.30 P.M.)

a
calf's
head
sauce gribiche
pour it on
a childhood pleasure
the creamy white brain
a nano *haut-le-coeur*
(heart rises to brain to speak its mind)
at the circumvolutions (? check
dictionary — months of French
overlay English — instability of
vocabulary — shimmy back & forth —
love your false friends — the words
migrate in all seasons — as word
for all reasons? — spice up your
vagrant vocables — *scheinheilige* —
where does that German word
come from, now, here, at la Grille,
the grille, the lattice work, whispered
through the monkish grate at
back of mind by childhood
prompter, or Celan's speech-grille?
((*Eisheiliger, Eisbein, Eiswein*
or is it the ¼, un quart
Pouilly-Fuissé speaking *(schein-*
heilig)
        sheen-holy,
the brain, the brain = a childhood taste
on toast with black
butter & capers, fork-mashed mother's treat
— or medical school shiver, cut
-ting into soft tissue, an organ
(ogre) held in — fitting, filling —

both hands, shaky pudding
thumbs on "foramina" (*sulcus*
is that the word, *sulcus terminalis*,
a furrow twice explored — slight shiver
helps knife — as if it needed it —
slice through non-resistant tissue,
careful/careless share — to eat
everything (a pig, well-used
is 450 servings snout to tail
a pig is *haram* in Beirut & Darfur,
I am ashamed as I shiver
through he brain — the one on the
plate, or the one in its case, this skull? —
a shiv, romantic twitch
in an imagined *zigeuner* underground
the blubbery cheek — black skin
(Miles called it green on the
pintade's armpit, refused to
eat, a shudder bigger, more
intractable than my shiver —
shudder of the unknown as
against shiver of history (personal
repetition) easily overcome by
mouth pleasure, tongue in slomo
crushes soft slice against top of
the mouth, palate palace
roof & last sip.
lean back.

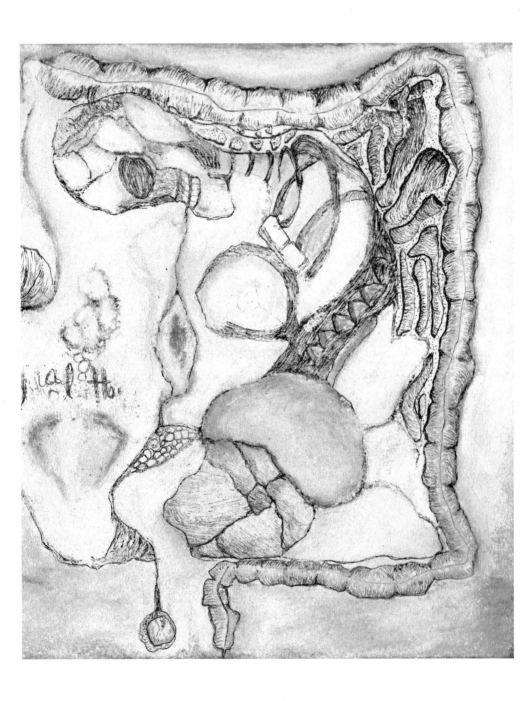

THERE ARE WAYS and then there are

no ways to make this wider or lay it

waste a countrified page a landscaped

country paged & thumb tacked to desperation

old chasm glimmers green barbiturate death

the care of the successful is indignation at

the world. the calluses

scream to heaven for

revenge of one order or another

but there are no ways there

is no take out in that place

only hell answers your late night calls

months later as the weather has changed

your appetite and your appetite

has not changed the world a hell

of a lot of bundles have shown up

eagerly masterless, carefree & scrumptiously

starved near death, the very image of

western beauty collapses into Darfur death

we will never learn you say or forgo another round

way to make this page wider

BLURB FOR HÜTTE

The building of thought

The making of thought dwells in
the building it is in

[building — dwelling — thinking

a questioning of the provincialism *revendiqué* by H.
a demythologizing
a gainst "grim fascination" with the hut

Here's a backdoor way —
revealing, modest, straight —
into Heidegger's Hütte, from the
ground plan. to the higher
reaches of the philosopher's
thought,

The importance of the place,
qua physical locale, where
thinking — even the most abstract
thought — happens cannot be
underestimated.

another keep
that keeps the world at critical distance
from H — this is no fawning laudatio

READING EDMOND JABÈS

Here, the end of the word, of the book, of chance.

Desert!
Drop that dice. It is useless.

Here, the end of the game, of resemblance.
The infinite, by the interpretation of its letters
Denies the end.

Here, the end cannot be denied. It is infinite.

Here is not the place
Nor even the trace.

Here is sand.

PAPYRUS

(probably the corner of a page ripped somehow from one of
Guillaume Apollinaire's erotic novels).

recto — prob. p. 311)

eked into my sisters'
   wasn't there. I noticed
    e Elise and my aunt
     ough a crack in my

         fanny was audible
        Now, drop your
          with your black

         Arms up in the
         arms. Look at

verso — prob. p. 312)

self the
trembling. I moved
groped at her slit.
"Let's be husband
   My finger played
went out of her,
were as white as
gently towards
pagne she had
on my rod and
pleasure was too
swelled. I move
teats. Then I
haunches and

Letter to Steichen's Ed

*In fact, every photograph is a fake from start to finish, a purely
impersonal, unmanipulated photograph being practically impossible.*
— Edward Steichen

Leiwen Ed,

Ech wees net ops du ons Sproch nach gekannt hues,
that's why I'll address you in American English.

You were born zu Béiwen, bei Roeser, in Luxembourg,
I was not
You were an American citizen,
I am still not,
I am just a plain citizen of Luxembourg.

You believed in the family of man
I am weary of families of any order and species.

But you are family
in that photo by Dana those clear blue
Luxembourg eyes exactly like cousin Lol's, the cut
of the face too, there's a resemblance, close to
the bone, close to the farm
a way in which the head
is held. High & loose. You're my home-
boy of old, Ed, a
cousin, maybe even
"cousin germain"
as the French wld say?

Now, you burned your paintings
when your gardener imitated one of yours —
a strange act, a criticism of

224 Pierre Joris

the representation of representation, maybe?
Or just a cheap trick to prove Duchamp wrong
for saying "stupide comme un peintre"
& move on to the new technologies?

Now, I never burned a single poem
have kept them all,
but then you had Carl Sandburg
in the family, devoted companion
for long walks & writing for you

I have always hated taking
photos but bought a camera at sixty
to shoot landscapes
& the family of one Joris
& half a dozen friends
but I always leave it home
or forget that it is in my pocket.

You were a famous delphinium breeder
I only brood over words
make poems & make anthologies,
weird cut flower bouquets

I am in Albany NY & sometimes
visit Buffalo where
you did avant-garde color autochromes
the year Ford introduced the model T-Ford
and one year after Picasso painted
his *Demoiselles*.

Ah the autochrome!
Hot off the 1903 minds
of the Frères Lumière,
them I've seen the Light Brothers,
first marketed in our year 1907,

it is an additive method
a process involving millions
of microscopic
grains of potato starch
(did you ever think of
the Luxembourg staple
food, *d'gromper,* when you
loaded the camera?)
dyed
bright blue-violet,
bright orange-red
& Kelly green
dusted on a slightly concave piece of glass
already coated with liquid pitch mixed
with a dram of beeswax
to keep it "tacky"
the random spaces filled with lamp-black
& a panchromatic silver halide emulsion

the resultant screen
was stochastic in nature
a random array
an abstraction way beyond the *Demoiselles'*
demure cubism
though the light you let
pass through the photo-sensitive plate
coming off
your "subjects", say Charlotte
Spaulding in Buffalo,
with the starch grains remaining as aligned
as the starch of her lacy dress
organized this randomness into
plain Edwardian beauty.

Ed, you were not Edwardian,
you were just a Luxembourg lad

in America who made good
& moved with ease between
Condé Nast & this here place,
fifty years before Warhol.
If I am trying so hard to
understand this autochrome process
(of which you said " no medium
can give me color of such
wonderful luminosity")
it is because you also said:

"If you don't take doors off their hinges,
how are you going to know
to put doors back on their hinges?"

Though that, cousin Ed,
may be where we disagree:
why put the doors back on
the hinges,
beauty will bolt anyway,
and all we are ever left with
is the beauty of doing the work,
the handwork, the hands on work,
your plates, my words.

Merci, cousin,
'daz gut ze wessen
daz du hei wars virun mir.

I like the imp
in impossibility
that makes it all
possible

In Praise of Pinot Blanc

Oh, you natural clone of a
Red clone, you are a most
Sympathetic Frankenstein,
High acidity signs your dif-
Ference with ubiquitous &
Sanctimellifluous chardonnay
—You are no poor man's
White Burgundy, you are de-

Lightful plum- & plump-
Ness, you're rich, ripe, juicy
Fruity apply & balmy on any 1
Of the 365 days of the year.
You're a sonnet in my heart
& the heart of my long sonnet
: come fill my glass, fill my
Mind, clone my soul with
Your heart, oh Pinot Blanc!

48 Words, found, somehow:

"the pen wrote me, the right hand and the knee" as one copy of
part of the Iliad signs off.

we now strongly suspect that this is the case for apes, dolphins
and, most recently, Asian elephants.

rationality plays little role in human snap decisions to act
altruistically

THE AUTOPOETIC PATH
   self regulating
      coming in your own mouth
      Uroboros
         creation swallowed

there is need for difference
   for the other, the gasp
      in between you and me
         something unknown
         a self that is not

the one I know
   so that the one I grasp
      could be
         the elf of someone's self.

ANTON WEBERN RETURNS FROM HUNGARY

gy other profusely brekker sabbatical napra storms in the world.
Am I bibs here In America the blacker, you've been watching, as
soon as the skyscape pinkish became, salmon-coloured busk, the
Catskills above swing. This time plus the informations.   Ez this
time also information. There is not more information & the total
yet today overnight dreams also forget The night-time information
, the night-time , which coolness place forty towards from our body
, n? kr? l ygur dream fiatalokról , chit fiends , one spit chain of
events sustorgása ama other world as far as that already not work
unless in our sleep not the snake however Kékulé or Delawares
brute already ekkor nor visit plus. Try memory & nothing neither
betide the recollection magát excepting. I came the snow & off also
t? nt neither I did not see him neither I can't hear but sensate in
my head it's snowing simply the phantasy the jeti elt? nt foot-mark
that's gone? nt in the snow. poke dve ta - pogatózva , but hey-day
mi towards Yet more morning , come in again the snow , the sun-
shine towards it was snowing , south towards , already too quickly
also , Earl Grey - sort in the evening , one rifle - shooting toss véget
the war Anton Webern backwards - plummets   Gondolj to that ,
aki humidor fired & ekkor thay killed. For what gondolhatott from
the house step out , humidor light , they're dying? Something mu-
sic thing could it have been or house fracas or only one félmosoly
wherefore soon san vége the war? Whether which thought about
during vein the death upon she's riding afterwards one perpetuity
through?   Zongorahangok , slope scale Bagolyhuhogás the black
key k between. square Multiply scopes , squall adjacent rooms THE
humoursome , mourning - your dress mind to hear surmise some-
thing , so call me , descant   Hideg descant. Cool December morn-
ing. north-east l north-east white contrail the nonsensical bluer
through. There is not other , only the oblivion memorable

READING ROTHSCHILD &

then so rudely interrupted
as I have to run to catch
the N train at 36th
to try to make St. Marks
I am late the train is
late too I am irritated the
train is too & apologizes
for being slow so I pull
Theogony out & start to read
with notebook at the
ready now the young Asian
girl next to me takes
her earphones out to listen to
the train's apologies &
her eyes fall on the open
Theogony & I notice
from the corner of mine
that she keeps reading
& all of a sudden she
smiles & starts to giggle before
putting her hand over
her mouth & turning away
still smiling & chuckling
& that's the best review
I could never write of
Dug's book, just then the
train stops at 14th street I
get off walk fast in fading
sun & nearly make it on
time to the Jack Spicer table
ronde no longer worried, in
fact happy, thinking how
great that just now as I move
back to NYC for the

first time since 1972
how great that there is a poet
here as sharp on the city
& as good on us as
my friend Paul Blackburn
was back then and now I'm
here at the Poetry Project
& of course Douglas is
here too listening to
what the West Coast people
have to say in NYC so I
close the notebook &
admire my man's
suspenders.

R.I.P. for C. L.-S.

The self is
"haïssable,"
detestable —

the man who just
lost his self
said

long ago
adding that
where there is

"pas de moi"
no me, no I

there will be
a nothingness

or an us,
no, he said "and"

"un rien et
un nous:"

which this morning
(pardon the departed)
I want to translate as

a noos
& a noose.

HOMAGE TO BADIA MASABNI

shift & tell
a rhythm travelled
along the silk
road from central
Asia going West
gone South
shifte telli
ah! Madame Masabni
you added violins,
cellos, accordions & ouds
to the traditional line-up
of riqq, derboukka, ney or zurna —

& the girls, the girls
now shift across the silk stage
& their tell-tale arms
move the story along
snake arms & veils
(probably seen in Isadora's
Paris shows)
and the belly was
now only one mooring,
moving part
    from East to
West & back
shivering
  the spine of the
Urals.

RoToR RESPONSE

But the emperor
because he had clothes
first disrobed

then fell
in the water
between (between,

always between
a barzakh
of seasons

the emperor was
summer his queen
sings

"injune" yourselves
there & here
your

Decembrists hop
scotch
archipelagoes of

must, wet embers
dark gloss on
etymo-dances

that saxophone
sears the waters
of the bay

fold the news
paper back to Teton
lands where

news is made by
Oglala gangs, like the
Nomads, cut

it up on the
reservation with
the Wild Boyz, TBZ

& Indian Mafia, the last
emperor — Max —
long ago shot

outside Mexico at
Cerro de las Campanas
in Querétaro

(Otomi for "place of
the ball game",
or P'urhépecha for

"place of
the great city" where there
are no great cities)

on high dry plains
where the only
way to travel

far, to leave the
terminal reservation
lock-up

is suicide, solo or
abetted — I
return to the coast

prefer Queens
for a ball game in a mis-
spelled city field

now home where Mount
Fuji's tethered
in front of my

eyes slightly to
the south of
Bow Sirius,

another tanker, with
Volunteer and Yves
(not Max)

Jacob half a mile
to the North in these
Narrows

again and again
to unload and
fill your tank

you got to
you got to
get out of this room.

THIS TANKER...

...has a tall house
on its stern — six stories
of lit windows just before
dawn. But now first
light has turned them off
on the Salacgriva, the
mouth of the Salaca, a town
in the Vidzeme region of
northern Latvia. A reversed
anchor in its coat of arms,
though what we need is a
new *mappe mundi* that is
more than just a Google map,
especially one that plays at
geopolitics and may restore a great
white place where China was.
But history, as much as geography,
does play such tricks on us
as soon as your back is turned —
whoever "you" may be in this or
any similar case. There is a
suggestion, for example, that
early Bolsheviks were educated,
multinational and ambitious.
Lenin's family, we learn this morning,
maybe a bit too late, some would say,
just as the tanker hauls in its
anchor to start moving in the
direction of the open sea, while
it simultaneously happens that
"this," (I think I'd wanted to write)
pen, a *Begreen* precise V5, runs out
of ink, clung desperately (we're back

now with Lenin's family) to its
status on the lowest rung of the
Czarist aristocracy.
       Though today
this is a highly unlikely process
in the country that has the most sweeping
web filtering system in the world.
Meanwhile the Salacgriva (remember her?) has
moved from the middle window to the South
window. Hadopi, the French
agency in charge of a new anti-
piracy scheme, has been accused
of pirating the font used in its logo.
But if someone you live with is accused
of three acts of infringement, your whole
household is yanked offline and added
to a list of those it is illegal to
provide internet service to. I still have
not heard back from the elderly
Haitian poet who sent me email
two hours before the disaster struck.
Had we been in Rome we would
probably not have been able to get
tickets for the world première of
Henze's *Immolazione*. When
you liked the music used on the
documentary you watched before
falling asleep, you were pleased to
discover who the composer was.
You fell asleep more easily than I did
maybe because of the fear, anguish
and soccer in Africa, which could
remain unassimilable, if that is a
word, as part of a study on
"The Modern as experience." She

can't determine if its is a crying
or a laughing matter. But who
can, these days, I want to ask whoever
is listening. We're out of wine
and a rose is a tulip is an anemone.

Sour Birth

dear Anselm,
there may be a typo
in that poem:
the line "Just a sour birth"
should read
"Just as our birth"
unless the poem wanted it to be
the other way around.

DAY'S END RUN

a thumb's thickness the thickness
of red all along the western horizon,
eastern edge of an island they call Staten.

WINTER POEM

It is "Spring" lying out there
in mid-january in the middle
of the Narrows, quietly,
silently, riding at
anchor, an old tanker
with an optimistic name
and Pacific Innovator's hard
at its heels, I mean stern.

New Year Poem

from hearth-work
shoot fire-particles,
the swarm, the warm
animals dancing
circling
the flames.
warm-blooded fire-breath, thus
this round & dance
to work fire
from earth
to dance us into
a new year

WHAT I SEE:

treegrille with water plane
last light over an island
plane tree leaves, yellow,
"tremble" in November wind.

the light crawls
out of the sky,
the yellow stripes
turn a darker red

a ritual play as in
le rouge et le noir
the red and the black
by contrast blackens the land.

All will now be color
of land
soon enough soon enough
night falls.

red, darkish,
yellow, "pus-colored" yellow light, he said,
fights back
from the botanical park:

it is in vain
but tomorrow I'll go
and kiss your leaf.
should tomorrow come.

ON GOETHE'S FLYLEAF

the word wedge
out of dream
driven between
night & day
out of Rilke
again is *Zwie
spalt* sudden
shudder as to
how to not to
think on the
word's redun
dancy — i.e.
what would
it mean to
split something
into one?

2.

to the split
between your
legs single
no zwiespalt

SHAKESPEARE'S SONNET #71, RE-ENGLISHED AFTER PAUL CELAN'S GERMAN VERSION WITHOUT CONSULTING THE ORIGINAL:

You should, once I'm gone, mourn only as long
as you hear the bell, the dark one, from the tower;
as long as it needs to tell the world:
He who lived with you went to live with the worms.

This I write, but you, having read it,
forget who wrote it. For look — I love you:
I wish I'd never been on your mind,
for when you think of me, sorrow steals upon you.

You should let — once your gaze rests upon these words,
once I'm dust, dust & no longer —
love become what I became,
and my name, do not speak it again:

The world, wise-eyed, already looks for your tears,
me, now gone, with you to taunt.

TIME IS NEVER TIMELY

always it wobbles
(*die* Zeit, *le* temps)
between already
& not yet

R Train Spotting

young man
head shaven
pale serious mien
agingly punkish
reading deeply
in Spinoza's *Ethics*
from 59th Street
until he gets out
at Pacific, gone
before I can doff
my cap verbally
or even nod
approval.

EARLY MORNING TRAIL

how can I get
from seepage
to sea page
this morning
without leaving
this seeded page?

DEAR GEORGE,
Evening Tide is approaching & she
is a towing vessel towing nothing
but herself up the Narrows at 10:23 tonight
& she has neither three sails nor
a mind of her own —
Will the boat split apart you may well ask?
Moby D. won't tell me, so I guess
we'll have to guess, though you shouldn't bet
against me betting against it, I did check it out with
Vessel-tracker & we are more than cautiously
optimistic, I mean some things
are written down — and not only on water —
so we can know them for sure, you
for example, wrote:
born 1:32 A.M. July 14, 1942 White Plains N.Y.
and that makes sense
while I more recently wrote *And having a birthday that rhymes*
with the day of liberation of a stony prison, a Bastille, freeing
among others one mad writer — the marquis de Sade —,
can only induce a cautiously phantasmic sense of revolutionary
inevitability,
which doesn't make as much sense but is offered
here in the pleasure of a shared Bastille day b-day
& as you also proposed that if you
"could be born once a day for 44 years
perhaps I could metamorphose into a dolphin at 4:14 A.M.,
wolfhour" though it hasn't been 44 years since that poem
I'm looking forward to see you dolphining it
in a glad surround dance of the *Evening Tide.*

for George Quasha at 70
10.23 p.m. June 14, 2012, Sorrentinostan, N.Y.

IS IT A GOOD THING TO FIND
two empty pages between the day
before yesterday and yesterday
when trying to make room
for the blue opera afternoon of
today a sunday like any sunday
in may?
            there is no one could tell
or judge though my own
obsession with the in between
should dictate the answer
& thus let me rejoice at being able
to insert today between the
day before yesterday & yesterday
as if it were the yeast of night
allowed these spaces to open
(do not say holes to grow)
in the spongy tissue of this
my papery time-space discon-
tinuum.
            leaven of earth leaven of writing
of running writing to earth
in these inbetweenesses that now
pleases as much as the opera in ear
that asks que dieu vous le rende dans
l'autre monde but the desire is to stay right
here in this world this inbetween even as
the sound changes the radio sings son
vada o resti intanto non partirai
di qua
   exactly my feeling cosy on these
pages now filled and pushing up against
yesterday

TIME IS VEXING

We have passed midnight
by some twelve hours
and the question arises
are we late, are we early?

THE GULF (FROM RIGWRECK TO DISASTER)

A TRIPTYCH

1- Rigwreck / composer: Gabriel Jackson

Interlude: Word Swarm 1

2- Love at First Sight / composer: Chris Jonas

Interlude: Word Swarm 2

3- Dis/aster — Oildreck / composer: Gene Coleman

Commissioned by Donald Nally and The Crossing
with funds provided by the Pew Center for Arts & Heritage through the Philadelphia Music Project

Rigwreck

Pierre Joris (b.1946)

GABRIEL JACKSON

Duration: 15'

First performed by The Crossing, directed by Donald Nally, at the Presbyterian Church of Chestnut Hill, Philadelphia, on 30 June 2013 during The Crossing's 5th Annual Month of Moderns

OXFORD UNIVERSITY PRESS, MUSIC DEPARTMENT, GREAT CLARENDON STREET, OXFORD OX2 6DP

RIGWRECK

A THROW
      what do we know, what can we know?
        OF THE DICE
of science, of love?
           only the facts, that is to say
             only effects
               NEVER
can this happen
NEVER even if, can this happen
      in science, in love
        EVEN WHEN CAST
Indra's net of love,

EVEN WHEN CAST
           money's net of stone
what do we know, what can we know?
        What has caused this gulf
between water & oil, you & me
             IN ETERNAL CIRCUMSTANCES
      (no circumstances are eternal,
AT THE HEART OF
         of this rigwreck
What will we know?
      We know only effects / have to choose
the causes

A SHIPWRECK at the heart that the
gulf widens
         between water & oil, you & me
              fish & water, me & you
                   that the
                        Abyss
         between water & water, you & you
              me & me, oil & fish
widened then whitened
                   there is slack growing
              raging underwater in the heart
                        underheart in the water
         on the brain

what we know is oil & water don't mix
what we know is fish & oil don't mix

    what we know is you & I have to mix
    what we know is you & I have to live

        under an incline
      clinamen of a warming clime
an angle not an angel tells us
                me & you want to live
         even if despair desperately soars
    & gets an angry rise

from the phantom pain of its own planet's sore
                              broken wing
        a second-hand angel singing Ecce Homo,
                  Ecce Homo, though not so Sapiens,
conscious liar,
          beforehand relapsed, liar, liar,
                  not released from wrongly steering
                          the flight of this planetary love affair
                              no use repressing the outbursts
                                  of this lethal love affair
                                      cleaving the bounds

of this oily love affair
        at the root of greed
           set the rig afloat
                a ship finally a ship
                      the impossible change
for deep inside weighs the admission of impending disaster

the shadow hidden in the depth
      by this by this arrogance this arrogance
    at the root of greed this arrogance
      at the root of arrogance
        this love this love for more
            a more always spelled out in money

blows the rig up this morning
will blow the world up tomorrow
     there is no alternate sail
         ship earth in space / space ship earth
            the only raft for dumb sapiens
who has to learn to love
this imperfect raft
there is no alternate sail

dumb sapiens has to learn love
   has to learn to adjust
     has to learn to look to the spread
the spreading of disaster
   has to learn to jump
      its yawning depth
as great as any abyss
         between you & me
   the hull of a rig
    the hull of a ship

careening from side to side
      turns over & is for a moment cathedral
            burning church of the worship of money
brightly floating death flaunting love
              rigwreck rigwreck
a catastrophe here now,
         the circumstances local & global
     not eternal only this now
cannot grasp the hawser
           opens a gulf
              between life & death

a millimeter uncrossable
     a BP centipede monster
at the heart of this rigwreck
        abolish   abolish
abolished responsibility
       Moloch, Moloch
Moloch —
      rules, Moloch
              rules
all rules broken when Moloch rules.

Brockley, April-May 2013

INTERLUDE 1:

WORD SWARM APRIL 20 2010

joint military operation
Iraqi American forces killed two senior
al-Qaeda leaders
Abu Ayyub al-Masri, and Abu Omar al-Baghdadi
News broke explosion at 11 p.m. EST on BP's
Deepwater Horizon oil rig
safe house in Thar-Thar in the province of
Salaheddin
umbrella group, Islamic State of Iraq
radical Sunni militant groups
General Raymond Odierno said significant blow
to al-Qaeda
24 people killed 2 separate suicide bombing
attacks in Peshawar
A schoolboy victim attacks take death toll
to 73 in three days, after two blasts in the
city of Kohat killed 49 people during the
weekend
News broke an explosion occurred at 11 p.m.
EST on BP's Deepwater Horizon oil rig in the
Gulf of Mexico
A magnitude 5.2 earthquake hit Western
Australian mining town
Kalgoorlie-Boulder this morning.
Long Island teen guilty of murdering
Ecuadorian immigrant Marcelo Lucero.
Toyota pays a record $16.4 million fine to the
US government over allegations that the
automaker concealed defects in its vehicles
— sticky pedal
NATO service members died bomb attack army
base southern Afghanistan.

K

138

S1 SS/AA: In time, continuous 16th note pulse; each voice independent
    choose freely between cells; add in single-beat rests at liberty

S2

A1

A2 SS/AA DYNAMICS: Throughout this section, conductor conducts dynamics
    freely: includes a range from pp to ff with sudden and gradual
    changes.

T1

T2

B1

B2

LOVE AT FIRST SIGHT

CHOIR:

          THE MASTER is no master
      the master is a corp   a corpse a corporation
        beyond outworn calculations
where Moloch where Moloch arisen
             is a manoeuvre with age-
less scorn for you & me
      scorn for love / love forgotten
       the master is absent
now present here only Dewey
           could have gripped the helm once
upon a time & called his mates
     now locked into the assistant driller's shack's C chair
 can his love hear him

SOLO (Dewey's voice):
    Thirty years offshore
              & I can smell a rat
    leaving a rig, I can, I do right now —
I'm toolpusher, not master,
       should sleep but follow
            inauspicious orders
tomorrow's another day, night's growing darker
       something's wrong here, something's off
           shouldn't follow inauspicious orders
     It is night / the only light
         is tomorrow is Sheri
Sheri my love a gulf between us
      my message reaches across a gulf
          awaits you listen listen
             left it this morning at first light
O why am I not ashore I knew
      the bosses would lie would cut
           corners until from this conflagration...

CHOIR:

        at his feet mud overflows the rig floor
            shoots through the derrick
    the blowout preventer does not act
the well's blown out
    Dewey dead now in this conflagration
on the no way unanimous horizon
        end of the horizon
            of the deepwater horizon
a Gulf prepares itself
    the fist would grip it
   will swallow the tossed & burning rig

as one threatens destiny and the winds, the elements all
        eleven die
   the one Number which can be no other
      eleven die
        their Spirit hurled
                into tempestuous fire gas explosions
      nothing can seal the gap nothing can go proudly
   eleven die
love left ashore a Gulf
             between their loves & their corpses
     eleven die
       eleven die.

SOLO (Female Voice/ Sheri):

    Dewey got pretty hot
      Dewey never—ever—ever
        loses his temper — never, ever, ever.
   If he really believed this could have happened,
     he'd never, never let them do it.
Calls at 9 a.m. each morning
    missed his call that morning,
      phone didn't ring, he left
        a message I deleted as
   I knew he was coming home
     knew he was coming home.

CHOIR:
    Don't hesitate
        cut off from the secret they withhold
            cadavers that will not wash ashore
caught rather than dressed
        now in shrouds of lethal
    oil & dispersant pearls
old madmen play the game on behalf of the waves
        one surges over the chief toolpusher
    a directly shipwrecked

all-American love story flows over:
        of the man no submissive graybeard
          who just liked being home,
    ancestrally huntin', fishin', playin' on his tractor
        not to unclench his hand
She without a ship
    a small place in Ohio, no matter where vainly there was:
        K-mart in walking distance,
            mall twenty minutes by car.
They met when he drove up to the local Kerr
    gas station where Sheri worked.

SOLO (Female Voice /Sheri):
It was love at first sight
    We had the old time Coca-Cola coolers.
        He reached in for one he was sittin' there
            we were talkin' that was it...
                He had this smile. It would make you melt.
                Love at first sight.

CHOIR:
      Contracted before & above the worthless wellhead showed
She was 18 & he was 21 when they got married
             an all-American love story
                  the legacy of his disappearance
        yet back then no gulf between them
            to some unknown the ulterior immemorial demon.

SOLO (Female Voice):
It was love at first sight.
When we got married so young
everyone was looking for a baby.
There wasn't one.
We were just in love.

CHOIR:

From dead & narrow lands
   induced / seduced
      by an old man toward this supreme lethal
        conjunction with probability
this morning she expected him home
    sister called at 5 a.m. said turn on the t.v.
      she knew right away that he'd be dead.
        Even his boyish shadow
caressed & polished, drained & washed
    not to return wave-softened
      unyielding bones stripped off
        lost among the debris

INTERLUDE 2:

WORDSWARM 20 APRIL 2010

death toll of foreign soldiers in 2010 to
166 in Afghanistan
McLaren driver Jenson Button won the
Chinese Grand Prix
re-open the skies over Europe
ash from a volcano in Iceland
a high pressure here and a low pressure there
News broke that an explosion occurred at 11
p.m. EST on BP's Deepwater Horizon oil rig
in the Gulf of Mexico southeast of Venice
the jet stream came down, spun around, &
then went back up through the Straits of
Gibraltar
amphibians, reptiles, mammals, bird and
fish species
Remembering Columbine 11 years ago
celebrate National Park Week
largest subtropical wildnerness
showdown Senate financial reform
Zephyrs top Express in 11 innings
Today's Money Word is deflation
BIG Oil Rig Explosion Off Louisiana Coast,
11 to 15 People Missing, Infernal Blaze
trust leaked away with the Tritium
bar NEPA analysis of climate change impact
Being fat is bad for your brain
erratic, potentially fatal heart rhythms
defibrillator responsibility the Guidant
Corporation
short-circuit and fail
"Nobody is being held accountable."

Google criticized privacy practices
the privacy rights of the world's citizens
forgotten
stricter enforcement of title IX
Twain's last words
Best Nonholiday Quarter for Apple
Taliban sniper fire lethality rates drop
Peter Steele "Life is killing me" is dead
no ban on animal cruelty videos
Off Louisiana Coast, 11 to 15 People Missing,
Statoil Committed to Oil Sands
Bush warcrimes on off broadway
Miami Condo Sales rise
Oil Rig Explosion Infernal Blaze
boxer hangs himself in jail
Reds pitcher Volquez suspended
Tuesday, April 20
News broke that an explosion occurred at 11
p.m. EST
on BP's Deepwater Horizon oil rig in the
Gulf of Mexico
52 miles southeast of the Louisiana port of
Venice.
According to the Coast Guard, 11 to 15 crew
members were reported missing
of the total 126 workers aboard the rig
at the time of the blast.

Carta NO. 23
MANUSCRIPT PAPER

Dis/Aster — Oildreck

Disaster: not thought gone awry

when all this first started
   my body broke out into real bad rashes
      my eyes my face my neck my chest my back my shoulders
big giant holes on the back of my legs,
   holes the size of a #2 pencil
      looked just like the holes
         in the fish
            in the lab
               on the screen

Gulf: from Greek κόλπος **(kólpos) m. [masculine], a bosom, from Proto-European *bheu-ə- : "to swell, bend, curve"**

WHAT HAVE YOU DONE TO KNOW DISASTER?

we went to detox —December 11 to January 12
the children feel much better now
Alina still has bad days
she may never be 100%.
my little boy is doing fantastic,
my husband's better &
I'm feeling better too…
I've shelled out $40,000

GULF: A HOLLOW PLACE IN THE EARTH

DISASTER IS ON THE SIDE OF FORGETTING

we did blue crab before BP
         but since BP
                  we don't blue crab anymore

GULF: AN ABYSS, A BOTTOMLESS OR UNFATHOMED DEPTH

Disaster: Care for the Minuscule

all of a sudden we had shrimp
    with what they call black gill disease
        if they were blue would it be blue gill disease?
we've had shrimp
    with growths on them
        we've had fish with growths on 'em

Gulf: A deep Chasm, a steep-sided rift, gap or fissure, a large difference of opinion

DISASTER: SOVEREIGNTY OF THE ACCIDENT

the Vietnamese & the Cambodian communities
  a really tough time being hired on
    the great language barrier:
      90% of the information put out
        in the first 60 days was English only

**GULF: A BASIN, FROM LATIN "BACCA" WINE JUG, WELCH "BAICH,"
LOAD, BURDEN, IRISH "BAC," HINDRANCE**

In relation to disaster, one dies too late

the herring came in to mature
        dropped on the seafloor dead
compromised immune system couldn't
        fight off a parasite, a natural bacteria

Gulf: a rock formation scooped out by water erosion

DISASTER DISORIENTS THE ABSOLUTE

grey amberjack, king mackerel, red snapper, mangrove snapper,
caught off shore when we gutted
        had black sludge inside their stomachs
      crossed stomach walls
        made holes in the meat
you could literally physically see it with the naked eye

GULF: (OBSOLETE) THAT WHICH SWALLOW, THE GULLET

DISASTER COMES AND GOES

the blue runners will hit the oil
off the top of the water, the droplets,
larger fish get it inside of them eating
their normal food source and then
it's gone, it's gone it's not there anymore, it doesn't exist

GULF: THAT WHICH SWALLOWS IRRETRIEVABLY, A WHIRLPOOL, A SUCKING EDDY

DISASTER: NOMAD DISARRAY

the whole circle of life
in the Gulf things that we don't eat
        whales dolphins turtles all this different stuff
if it kills everything then what do we do?

    an overflow, people flooding
        the area all the way from Arkansas & all over the US
and they were able to come down here with boats
    because they weren't from here,
        they took some of our fishermen & put them over in
Alabama
        & took some Alabama fishermen & put them over here.
And what it was all about was
        controlling the images!

GULF: A LARGE DEPOSIT OF ORE (ROCK CONTAINING METAL OR GEMS) IN A LODE (A VEIN OF ORE IN BOUNDARIES, A RICH SUPPLY, ALSO SEE WATER-COURSE, LODESTONE, LODESTAR)

DISASTER MEANS TO BE SEPARATED FROM ONE'S STAR

if everybody got up and said "enough is enough"
— there is power in numbers —
then we may be able to move
& really get it cleaned up —
— it is still leaking
— mine said they ran through oil all day yesterday
oil & dispersant
in the water the dispersant
when they first put it out looked
like sand from the Sahara desert
into contact with the oil it gets foamy slimy nasty
on top of the water

GULF: FROM GREEK χόλπος (kólpos) m. [masculine], ANATOMICALLY, VAGINA AND/OR ATRIUM OF THE HEART

DISASTER LIES ON THE OTHER SIDE OF DANGER

DARK DISASTER CARRIES THE LIGHT

TAKES CARE OF EVERYTHING

Note: — The first two sections of the work are a partial writing-through of Stéphane Mallarmé's poem "A Throw of the Dice," using both Daisy Alden & my own translations. That poem, despite being usually called the first "abstract" poem of the modern avant-garde, does tell a story: that of a shipwreck and the drowning of its captain.

— A number of the spoken phrases in the second section are taken from interviews with Sheri Revette by Antonia Juhasz in the latter's book *Black Tide* (Wiley, 2011), talking of her husband, Dewey Revette, a driller killed in the Deepwater Horizon disaster on April 20, 2010. Sheri tells the story of their love and life together and the moments after Sheri's discovery of her husband's death.

— Chris Jonas at some point asked me for "news chatter," a "word swarm," scattered words not in the poem as such but yet relevant that he could use to make sounds with. I have gathered my gleanings of news chatter into two ticker tape-like "Interludes" inserted between the sections of the sequence.

— In the third poem, the spoken words in italics are taken from an interview I conducted in New Orleans in February 2012 with Kindra Arnesen, fisherwoman, wife of a fisherman, mother, activist, cofounder of the Coastal Heritage Society, a feisty & powerful voice in the fight for justice after the Gulf disaster, as willing to take on local prejudices as the BP or the US government.

— The texts of the bold-faced "frames" around her words use disaster definitions/pairings from Maurice Blanchot's book *L'écriture du désastre*, & etymological definitions of the word "gulf" from various dictionaries.

ADDITIONAL TITLES BY PIERRE JORIS

POETRY

Meditations on the Stations of Mansur al-Hallaj Chax Press
(2013)
Learn the Shadow (2012)
The Tang Extending from the Blade (2010)
Aljibar & Aljibar II (2007, 2008)
Routes, not Roots (Audio CD, 2007)
Meditations on the Stations of Mansur Al-Hallaj 1–20 (2006)
The Rothenberg Variations (2004)
Permanent Diaspora (2003)
Poasis: Selected Poems 1986–1999 (2001)
h.j.r. (1999)
out/takes (1999)
Winnetou Old (1994)
Turbulence (1991)
The Irritation Ditch (1991)
Janus (1988)
Breccia: Selected Poems 1972–1986 (1987)
Net/Work (1983)
The Book of Luap Nalec (1982)
Tracing (1982)
Hearth-Work (1977)
Antlers I–XI (1975)
Another Journey (1972)
The Fifth Season (1972)

ESSAYS

Justifying the Margins (2009)
A Nomad Poetics (2003)
Global Interference (1981)
The Book of Demons (with Victoria Hyatt) (1975)

TRANSLATIONS

Breathturn into Timestead: The Collected Later Poetry of Paul Celan (2014)

Bernat Manciet: Ode to James Dean with Nicole Peyrafitte (2014)

Exile is My Trade: A Habib Tengour Reader (2012)

The Meridian: Final Version—Drafts—Materials by Paul Celan (2011)

Jukebox hydrogène de Allen Ginsberg (2008)

Paul Celan: Selections (2005)

Lightduress by Paul Celan (2005)

The Burial of the Count of Orgaz and other Writings of Pablo Picasso (2004)

The Malady of Islam by Abdelwahab Meddeb (2003)

4X1: Works by Rilke, Tzara, Duprey & Tengour translated by Pierre Joris (2002)

Threadsuns by Paul Celan (2000)

Crystals to Aden by Michel Bulteau (2000)

The Sandals of Empedocles by Habib Tengour (1999)

Breathturn by Paul Celan (1995)

pppppp: The Selected Writings of Kurt Schwitters (1993)

From the Desert to the Book, Interviews with Edmond Jabès (1989)

The Unavowable Community by Maurice Blanchot (1988)

Lune faucon de Sam Shepard (1987)

Motel Chronicles de Sam Shepard (1985)

Sentiments éligiaques américains de Gregory Corso (1977)

Mexico City Blues de Jack Kerouac (1977)

Temporal Flight by Jean-Pierre Duprey (1976)

Chants de la Révolution de Julian Beck (1975)

Contretemps à temps de Carl Solomon (1974)

ANTHOLOGIES

    The University of California Book of North African Literature
        (vol. 4 in the *Poems for the Millennium* series), with
        Habib Tengour (2012)

    The University of California Book of Modern & Postmodern Poetry
        (vol. 1 & 2 of the *Poems for the Millennium* series), with
        Jerome Rothenberg (1995 & 1998)

    Poésie Internationale : Anthologie with Jean Portante (1987)

    Matières d'Angleterre with Paul Buck (1984)

EDITOR

    A Voice Full of Cities: The Collected Essays of Robert Kelly with
        Peter Cockelbergh (2014)

    Claude Pélieu: La Crevaille (2008)

    Paul Celan : Selections (2005)

    Joy! Praise! A Festschrift for Jerome Rothenberg on the Occasion
        of his Sixtieth Birthday (1991)

BLACK WIDOW PRESS

TRANSLATION SERIES

A Life of Poems, Poems of a Life by Anna de Noailles. Translated by Norman R. Shapiro. Introduction by Catherine Perry.

Approximate Man and Other Writings by Tristan Tzara. Translated by Mary Ann Caws.

Art Poétique by Guillevic. Translated by Maureen Smith.

The Big Game by Benjamin Péret. Translated with an introduction by Marilyn Kallet.

Capital of Pain by Paul Eluard. Translated by Mary Ann Caws, Patricia Terry, and Nancy Kline.

Chanson Dada: Selected Poems by Tristan Tzara. Translated with an introduction and essay by Lee Harwood.

Essential Poems and Writings of Joyce Mansour: A Bilingual Anthology. Translated with an introduction by Serge Gavronsky.

Essential Poems and Prose of Jules Laforgue. Translated and edited by Patricia Terry.

Essential Poems and Writings of Robert Desnos: A Bilingual Anthology. Edited with an introduction and essay by Mary Ann Caws.

EyeSeas (Les Ziaux) by Raymond Queneau. Translated with an introduction by Daniela Hurezanu and Stephen Kessler.

Fables in a Modern Key by Pierre Coran. Edited and translated by Norman R. Shapiro. Color illustrations by Olga Pastuchiv.

Furor and Mystery & Other Writings by René Char. Translated and edited by Mary Ann Caws and Nancy Kline.

Guarding the Air: Selected Poems of Gunnar Harding Translated and edited by Roger Greenwald.

The Inventor of Love & Other Writings by Gherasim Luca. Translated by Julian & Laura Semilian. Introduction by Andrei Codrescu. Essay by Petre Răileanu.

Selected Prose and Poetry of Jules Supervielle Translated by Nancy Kline, Patricia Terry, and Kathleen Micklow.

La Fontaine's Bawdy by Jean de La Fontaine. Translated with an introduction by Norman R. Shapiro.

Last Love Poems of Paul Eluard. Translated with an introduction by Marilyn Kallet.

Love, Poetry (L'amour la poésie) by Paul Eluard. Translated with an essay by Stuart Kendall.

Pierre Reverdy: Poems Early to Late. Translated by Mary Ann Caws and Patricia Terry.

Poems of André Breton: A Bilingual Anthology Translated with essays by Jean-Pierre Cauvin and Mary Ann Caws.

Poems of A.O. Barnabooth by Valéry Larbaud. Translated by Ron Padgett and Bill Zavatsky.

Poems of Consummation by Vicente Aleixandre. Translated by Stephen Kessler.

Préversities: A Jacques Prévert Sampler Translated and edited by Norman R. Shapiro.

The Sea and Other Poems by Guillevic. Translated by Patricia Terry. Introduction by Monique Chefdor.

To Speak, to Tell You? Poems by Sabine Sicaud. Translated by Norman R. Shapiro. Introduction and notes by Odile Ayral-Clause.

FORTHCOMING TRANSLATIONS

Boris Vian Invents Boris Vian: A Boris Vian Reader Edited and translated by Julia Older.

Earthlight (Claire de Terre) by André Breton. Translated by Bill Zavatsky and Zack Rogrow. (New and revised edition.)

The Gentle Genius of Cécile Périn: Selected Poems (1906–1956). Edited and translated by Norman R. Shapiro.

Reality and Desire (La realidad y el deseo): New Selected Poems of Luis Cernuda. Edited and translated by Stephen Kessler.

MODERN POETRY SERIES

ABC of Translation by Willis Barnstone

An Alchemist with One Eye on Fire by Clayton Eshleman

Anticline by Clayton Eshleman

Archaic Design by Clayton Eshleman

Backscatter: New and Selected Poems by John Olson

Barzakh (Poems 2000–2012) by Pierre Joris

The Caveat Onus by Dave Brinks

City Without People: The Katrina Poems by Niyi Osundare

Concealments and Caprichos by Jerome Rothenberg

Crusader-Woman by Ruxandra Cesereanu. Translated by Adam J. Sorkin. Introduction by Andrei Codrescu.

Curdled Skulls: Poems of Bernard Bador. Translated by the author with Clayton Eshleman.

Endure: Poems by Bei Dao. Translated by Clayton Eshleman and Lucas Klein.

Exile is My Trade: A Habib Tengour Reader. Translated by Pierre Joris.

Eye of Witness: A Jerome Rothenberg Reader Edited with commentaries by Heriberto Yepez and Jerome Rothenberg.

Fire Exit by Robert Kelly

Forgiven Submarine by Ruxandra Cesereanu and Andrei Codrescu

from stone this running by Heller Levinson

The Grindstone of Rapport: A Clayton Eshleman Reader

Larynx Galaxy by John Olson

The Love That Moves Me by Marilyn Kallet

Memory Wing by Bill Lavender

Packing Light: New and Selected Poems by Marilyn Kallet

The Present Tense of the World: Poems 2000–2009 by Amina Saïd. Translated with an introduction by Marilyn Hacker.

The Price of Experience by Clayton Eshleman

The Secret Brain: Selected Poems 1995–2012 by Dave Brinks

Signal from Draco: New and Selected Poems by Mebane Robertson

FORTHCOMING MODERN POETRY

An American Unconscious by Mebane Robertson

Disenchanted City by Chantal Bizzini. Edited by Marilyn Kallet.

Essential Poetry (1964–2015) by Clayton Eshleman

Funny Way of Staying Alive by Willis Barnstone

The Hexagon by Robert Kelly

Memory by Bernadette Mayer

Soraya (Sonnets) by Anis Shivani

LITERARY THEORY / BIOGRAPHY SERIES

Clayton Eshleman: The Whole Art Edited by Stuart Kendall.

Revolution of the Mind: The Life of André Breton by Mark Polizzotti

FORTHCOMING

Barbaric Vast & Wild: A Gathering of Outside and Subterranean Poetry (Poems for the Millennium, vol 5) Edited by Jerome Rothenberg and John Bloomberg

WWW.BLACKWIDOWPRESS.COM